Becoming a GOOD THING Before the RING

Rita Brooks

Wysdom Central
PUBLICATIONS, LLC
IGNITING A FLAME FOR GOD's WORD & GOD's WISDOM

©2021, Orethia Brooks

Published by Wysdom Central Publications, LLC
Columbia, South Carolina
Email: wysdomcentralpubs@gmail.com

Book cover design by danny_media
Printed in the United States of America

Scripture taken from the KJV are taken from the KING JAMES VERSION (KJV): KING JAMES VERSION, public domain.

Scripture quotations marked (NLT) are taken from the Holy Bible, New Living Translation, copyright © 1996, 2004, 2007 by Tyndale House Foundation. Used by permission of Tyndale House Publishers, Inc., Carol Stream, IL 60188. All rights reserved.

Scriptures taken from the Holy Bible, New International Version®, NIV®. Copyright © 1973, 1978, 1984, 2011 by Biblica, Inc.™ Used by permission of Zondervan. All rights reserved worldwide. www.zondervan.com The "NIV" and "New International Version" are trademarks registered in the United States Patent and Trademark Office by Biblica, Inc.™

DEDICATION

This book is dedicated to the two individuals who, without them, this book would not be possible. My fine, faithful, adoring husband who is worthy of all the favor this good thing has to offer. Thank you for being living proof of God's promise to me. You were worth waiting for.

To God the Father, Son, and Holy Spirit. Thank you for helping me find my real life in you. We love because you first loved us.

PROVERBS 18:22

Whoso findeth a wife findeth a good thing,
and obtaineth favour of the LORD.

TABLE OF CONTENTS

FOREWORD

What more can I say? It is an exciting time to see something my wife has poured her heart and soul into coming to fruition. Being a witness to the labor, prayer, and real-life experiences that went into making "Becoming a Good Thing Before the Ring" has been an extreme honor and to be honest, quite inspiring.

I remember when Rita told me God had placed it on her heart to write a book a while back. She explained her desire to help women grow in their relationship with Christ. She knew it would set them up to receive God's best for their lives in every area including marriage. She didn't know much about writing a book. All she knew was that she wanted to create something that reflected her journey to this place of understanding in God and empower others through her transparency to reach and even surpass that place as well.

Well, I am godly proud to say that she has done just that with "Becoming a Good Thing Before the Ring". This book will empower countless women to become a good thing not only for their future husbands but for themselves. Take it from the man who has seen the favor of God increase on my life because of the Good Thing I have found in my wife.

Rita, thank you for embodying all of the things you have written about. Congratulations baby, YOU DID IT!

I love you!

John Brooks

The Husband of Rita Brooks

INTRODUCTION

You are probably wondering who I am to tell you how to become a good thing before the ring. Well, I am a woman who at the age of 25 experienced a quarter-life crisis of sorts. I was knee-deep in a lifestyle that should have landed me in one of two places: jail or the grave. I know it sounds cliché, but it is the truth. I thank God, however, that He intervened, and gave me a different story. It was one that He had been trying to write for me all along.

I guess turning 25 and knowing that 30 is just around the corner would cause anyone to look up and want to reevaluate some things in their life. Partying, drinking, smoking weed, peddling drugs, all of those things were becoming old fast, and I knew that was not the kind of life I was meant for. When it was time to make changes, my flesh tried desperately to resist. My carnal nature wanted to do what it wanted to do, but every day I began making strides towards becoming a better version of myself including going on a 40 day fast to purge and get closer to God. I would love to say that a total transition happened right after that fast, but it didn't. However, by the time the fasting was over, I knew something was different about me. I was never the same again.

Life went on for a few more seasons when suddenly, the year following that fast, I decided that I was done being one foot in and one foot out of the Kingdom of God. It was silly of me to even think that one foot in and one foot out was even an option when it comes to the things of God. Jesus warns us about being lukewarm. He told the Sardis Church that because they were neither hot nor cold, He would spit them out of His mouth (Revelation 3:16). Ouch.

So one day, after hearing a pastor preach words that penetrated my soul, I answered the altar call before he could even extend the invitation for people to come down to give their life to Jesus. I felt convicted, yet not condemned. I had an overwhelming sense of hope, peace, joy, and love.

I have never looked back since that Sunday morning in 2012.

Instead, I decided to hide in God and chase after Him with all that I've got, and the result has been a life that was once only an elusive dream. Don't get me wrong, it hasn't always been butterflies and sunshine. After the initial honeymoon period of walking with the Lord (you know the one where everything is rosy and God seems to be answering every one of your prayers seemingly faster than you can even get them out), I entered what I like to refer to as my wilderness season. It was a season of sowing, tears, along with a lot of uncertainty. More was being required of me than ever before. I had given God a yes, but I had no idea that that one yes would cost me so much.

The thing about a wilderness season is the journey can last as short or as long as you make it. Take the children of Israel for example. They wandered around in that wilderness for 40 years on a journey that was only supposed to take 11 days. How does that even happen? I'll tell you how: an erroneous mindset. If you want to obtain all that God has for you, you will have to have the right mindset. Negative thinking, murmuring, fear, complaining, excuses, ungratefulness, laziness, covetousness- none of these things will cut it on the journey to your promised land. You have to make a conscious decision that you are going to let go of anything that is hindering you and dive headfirst into only those things that are going to launch you into your destiny.

The reason I believe my story is so powerful is that everything happened relatively fast. Looking back, it seems as if God redeemed the time and accelerated His plans for my life. Of course, it did not seem fast when I was living it out, but now that I am on the other side, I look back, and I am just amazed at how in just two short years I went from process to promise. I see so many people walking with the Lord for years and sometimes even decades going around the same mountain. It does not have to be this way. Don't misunderstand me. The timing of God is a factor. After all, He is Sovereign. Some things you just will not see until you enter a certain time and season of your life. However, many times we claim to be waiting on God and believing for this or that. We claim it, speak it, confess it, all the while failing to realize that we are holding up the promise. It could be something that we failed to do that we should have done or something that we are doing that we should not be doing. Maybe it's a test we can never seem to pass that keeps coming back up or an act of obedience we failed to follow through on. Whatever it is, the problem is us, not God or other people-we are the common denominator. This is a hard truth that I had to come to grips with when I realized that I was in the wilderness way longer than I wanted or needed to be.

I never thought that I would get married. Of course, I have always had the desire, but I didn't think marriage was something that I would actually attain. I could not fathom it. And even if by some chance I did become someone's wife, I figured it would be one of those shotgun weddings down at the courthouse as a way for my longtime boyfriend to oblige me after putting up with him and being his ride or die for almost a decade. This was my thinking B.C. (before Christ). After all, before moving to Atlanta, I had never even attended a wedding, let alone seen any examples of great marriages. However, once I decided to live for God, something deep down inside of me began to believe that I was someone's wife. I did not know when I would get married or to who, but for once in my life, I began to believe that having a happy, healthy marriage with a godly man was attainable for me. Yes me, the young girl from the inner cities neither raised by her mother or father. The girl who stayed in an abusive relationship for much longer than she should have. The girl who slept with more men outside of marriage than she would care to admit- yes ME. It was all possible through Christ. When I read in 2 Corinthians 5:17 that I was a new creature in Christ, that the old things had passed away, and that all things were made new, I believed it. I hid that Word in my heart and spoke it over my life anytime the enemy tried to spew his lies and tell me any different. This brings me to why I am even writing this book in the first place.

I truly believe that there is an attack on the covenant of marriage headed by our enemy, Satan. The concept of it, the sanctity of it, even individual marriages, I believe, is the target of his wiles. This is evident in the way the media portrays it and the way it is perverted every single day. One of the main reasons I believe it is being attacked in such a way is because marriage is supposed to be a picture of Jesus and His church- the bride and the bridegroom. The same way Jesus loves and laid down His life for His church is the same way a husband is called to love and lay down his life for his wife (Ephesians 5:25). Marriage is supposed to be an example of the strong, selfless, agape, Christ kind of love. It is a love that pursues, a love that endures, a love that commits, and a love that never fails. This world needs to see that type of love on display.

Another reason I believe marriage is being attacked is that Satan knows the value of having men in their rightful places in the home and family. Mark 3:27 says that no one can enter a strong man's house and plunder his goods unless he first binds the strong man. This demonstrates to us that the man is a valuable asset as the head and cornerstone of their families. I believe that many issues in society and especially with our youth could be remedied if men all over the world would begin to take their rightful place in the homes and be godly husbands and fathers. That scripture illustrates that to get to everything and everyone else in the home, the strong man must first be taken down. If there is no strong man present, everyone and everything in that house is left vulnerable and is susceptible to attack.

Did you know that you can accomplish more with a partner? Deuteronomy 32:30 says this: one man can chase a thousand, and two can put ten thousand to flight. Now math has never been my strongest subject, but it would seem to me that when two people come together for one cause, there is a lot more that can be done. Now, from what I've read about God in the Bible, He is the best businessman there is, and He's always looking to maximize and receive the best return on His investments. Take the parable of the talents (which symbolizes the Kingdom of God) outlined in Matthew 24:14-30, for example. When the person who was given one talent did not come back with a return on the investment, the master was not happy about it, and He even gave their talent away to the person who had the largest return on their investment. If there is one thing that I have learned about God over the last few years, it is that He is very purposeful. Nothing with Him is ever wasted. He does everything with intentionality, and so I try to keep this characteristic in mind whenever I am facing any circumstance. God always has an agenda, and the Bible tells us that it is His purpose and His plans that will prevail (Proverbs 19:21). So you're probably thinking "What does all of this have to do with my relationship status?" Well, a lot actually. Whether you are single or married, you have an important role in the Body of Christ if you are a believer. But, when two people come together in the covenant of marriage, God has a purpose for that couple to fulfill as one. He adds a special anointing and a certain grace as well as favor to see it come to pass. There is no other earthly union that is as strong and powerful on the earth as that of marriage. I am certain God could use more couples, who are filled with His Spirit and have a kingdom agenda to help do His will here in the earth.

I remember when my husband, John and I were just friends, and we attended the same small group at church. We had absolutely no idea that we would end up married, and we never even considered one another as a potential mate. Toward the end of one of our small group meetings, a woman had a prophetic Word. She stated that God was going to put two people together from our small group and they would eventually get married. She went on to say that they could not fulfill their purpose apart from one another, but that once they were married, they would be able to fulfill their God-given purposes together. I began to search the room with my eyes wondering who it could be, and I even tried to put people together in my head. As much as I wanted that Word to be for me, I just knew it couldn't be because I was not in any way, shape, or form interested in anyone in that room. In fact, I was convinced that my husband was outside of the four walls of that church. Well, boy was I wrong because John and I ended up dating and getting married less than 3 years later. God brought back this moment to my remembrance while John and I were engaged, and I was just amazed looking back at how it played out. God has a specific plan for each one of us, and while it may not necessarily mean that you and your husband will go into ministry together, it does mean that He has a specific purpose for your life and your union, and He expects you to carry it out.

So before you go any further in this book I want you to know that marriage was and is God's idea, and if it is a desire of your heart then it is available to you. Maybe, for whatever reason, you are having a difficult time believing that you could be someone's wife or that you can have a happy, healthy marriage. Maybe you have seen too many marriages fail or maybe you have just been waiting for so long that you are just about ready to give up. It could be that you have been physically, verbally, or emotionally abused and you feel as though you are too scarred. Maybe you have been married before or you have children out of wedlock or from a previous marriage. Whatever your circumstance, I want you to know that the marriage of your dreams is available to you. I pray that your hope and your strength will be renewed as you read the pages of this book and are reminded that marriage was God's idea, and He has not changed His mind about it or you. Furthermore, God does not want you to just get any old man or settle for any old marriage. This book is meant to empower you to have the kind of marriage that He intends for every one of His children who desires it. Almost anyone can get married, but God's will for you is a happy, healthy marriage that stands the test of time and that glorifies Him.

This book will challenge you in ways that may be uncomfortable or new to you, but that's a good thing. Allow yourself the opportunity to be challenged to see your desired results. You probably have heard it be said that to get something that you've never had before, you have to do something you've never done before. I truly believe that. You have tried it your way for years. It is now time you allow God to write your love story and show you how to become a good thing. You see, God did not give a husband as some sort of prize for good behavior. He was not rewarding me for following Him. Instead, my decision to follow Him and surrender my will and my ways for His, put me in alignment with His plan for my life that He already had the blueprint for before I was even born. So, allow yourself to cooperate, not frustrate, the plan of God for your life so that you too can walk fully into your destiny.

PART I

LET'S BUILD A FOUNDATION

CHAPTER 1

First Things First: Are You Ready?

Proverbs 18:22 states: He who finds a wife, finds a GOOD THING and obtains favor from the Lord. Notice that it says he who finds A WIFE. It does not say he who finds a girlfriend, boo, bae, side chick, or even woman. It clearly states he who finds a WIFE. This leads me to believe that being a wife is the state in which he finds her, not something that she magically becomes when he puts a ring on her finger the day of their wedding. Instead, I would submit to you that being a wife is a posture of the heart and is manifested in your actions before you ever say I do. Disclaimer: You are not married if you have not legally been joined together with your spouse and made a covenant before God so don't be out here doing married folks stuff if you haven't taken all those steps. Ok? Just thought I would provide some clarity given my previous statement. Going back to my point now is the time to prepare. Now is the time to carry yourself as such. I now realize God was preparing me and cultivating me through various seasons and situations in my life long before I was able to say that I was ready to be someone's wife. Do not waste these precious moments during your single season.

Learning to Love Well

We all have this idea of love and marriage in our heads. Certain images have been planted into our minds since we were young through different mediums such as movies, tv shows, songs, our familial relationships and background, and more recently, social media. Over time, our idea of love and marriage has been shaped and reshaped into whatever we think about it today. It may have even evolved into a fantasy of sorts. You may imagine what it will be like once you get married, waking up to the love of your life every single day, rolling over to kiss him good morning, and cuddling him throughout the night. Maybe you envision exotic trips and adventures with your life partner or building a family full of beautiful children. Maybe you envision starting traditions and celebrating the holidays or building an empire together with the love of your life. Or perhaps you can't wait to have someone to help take care of your needs and tell all your hopes, dreams and fears to. Maybe you're just looking for someone to love you and cherish you and give you everything that has seemed to be missing. It all sounds rather….romantic. Well, I hate to burst your bubble, but that's not what love and marriage are all about. Sure you will no doubt experience some of those things I mentioned, but that is by no means the gist of love and marriage. At the core of all of those images and fantasies is the desire to please yourself and to have your own needs met, but love- the agape, God kind of love that is required in a covenant relationship such as marriage is the complete opposite.

The kind of love that I am referring to says "What can I do for you?" rather than "What can you do for me?" Let me tell you a little story.

One day, I had a breakthrough in the middle of a Red Lobster restaurant. My now BFF (back then she was just a new friend), asked me to join her there one Sunday after dance practice. Initially, I had no intention of taking her up on the offer. Up until that point, we had been arguing for days about something that I don't remember the specifics of right now. I do remember however that it was exhausting, and I was ready to call it quits on our new friendship.

That was easy for me to do-call it quits on people. The second anyone did anything to hurt my feelings, annoy me, turn me off or even treat me too good, I wanted nothing else to do with that person. It was just easier for me to cut the person off and move on to the next. This trait spanned across almost all of my relationships whether it was a potential mate, a friend, an associate, and even some family members. Almost everyone was dispensable in my book. At first, I would cut them off in my mind. I would lose all interest as well as any semblance of emotion that I ever felt for them. It was quite cold now that I think about it. Most times, I would not even offer the courtesy of telling them or explaining what happened. I would simply begin to ignore them, decline any offers to spend time with them, and neglect to contact them until eventually, they got the picture. Now that I think about it even more, it was also quite immature of me.

So, that is what I had begun doing to my BFF. Little did she know, she was already cut off in my mind, and I was prepared to end the friendship altogether. It had just become too much for me. I hated conflict. I never had to deal with it because in my family we all just swept things under the rug. I was raised by my grandmother and grandfather, and while they did a phenomenal job taking care of me and my siblings, we were not a family who talked much about our issues. In my relationships, it was much of the same. There was no real communication, only surface conversations that masked deep problems. Going back and forth with her was extremely annoying and quite honestly I just did not care. I realize now how bad that sounds, but it was my truth back then. It was hard for me to care about situations and things because, over the years, I had built up a thick shell that I now recognize as a defense mechanism. In the past, I was hurt badly by someone close to me and so all other situations paled in comparison. At least, that's how it felt.

Nevertheless, after minutes of begging, I obliged and decided to join her at the restaurant (more for the meal than anything). As we began to rehash the details of the arguments from the previous few days, we realized that we fought a lot. The details of the situation were always different but the root, we realized was the same. At this point in our friendship, we had been fighting so much that we considered going in for a counseling session at our church. We just could not figure out how to stop all the bickering and move past the conflict. So finally my BFF had a brilliant idea to ask the Holy Spirit. It sounded so simple, yet it was so profound. Of course, the Holy Spirit could help us. He knows ALL things which means He knows what is at the root of all of these arguments, AND he knows how to fix it. He is all-knowing and full of wisdom. James 1:5 says "If any of you lacks wisdom, let him ask of God who gives to all liberally and without reproach, and it will be given to him."

By the time we were finished with our meal, we had written instructions from the Holy Spirit on a paper napkin. There were only two instructions of which one was for me and the other for my BFF. My instructions were to do in every circumstance, for my BFF what I knew she would want for me to do in that given situation even if I did not feel like it. For example, if she sends me a text and asks how is my day going, generally, I would give a one-word answer. It's not because anything is wrong, but because if my day is going well I would say just that with no elaboration. Well, my BFF is not here for the one-word answers. Instead, she wants a full synopsis and explanation complete with details. I knew that to be true, but I would still give one-word answers because I did not feel the need to change who I was for another person. You see, many times we are loving someone the way we want to be loved instead of loving them the way they need/want to be loved and that is selfish. We must take the time to truly love the people that God has gifted us with the way they need and desire to be loved. That is a part of loving someone well.

I remember so clearly being in the shower one day and hearing God speak to my heart. He said, "Rita, if you can't even keep, appreciate, and cultivate the relationships that I have already given you (referring to a group of friends I was in a big argument with), how do you expect Me to ever bring you a husband?" Ouch! God was right. Had I not checked that old attitude and mindset back then, I would have brought it into a marriage which would have been a recipe for disaster and a cause for many arguments. It could have even potentially led to a divorce. I can honestly say that I have a beautiful marriage. Not perfect, but beautiful and I truly believe a big part of that is because I learned how to love people the right way before entering into a covenant relationship. I have not arrived by any means, but I am so much better than where I used to be, and I will continue to let God guide me in all of my relationships.

So as simple as the instructions were, I knew that it would be a challenge for me. However, it was one that I was willing to accept. If we truly value a person, and if we love them like we claim to love them then we will do what it takes to make them happy and make them feel loved even if it is uncomfortable to our flesh. Whether it is a friend, boyfriend, husband, mother, sister, or whomever, we should choose to love them this way because that is what love does, it gives.

To be honest, the first few times I was challenged to do what I knew my BFF would appreciate was hard. I had to do what I like to call "faith it til I make it." Although it felt phony at the time, that is not what it is at all. It was actually me putting my flesh in check. I had to put a smile on my face and do things cheerfully that I did not necessarily want to do, but guess what? The arguments became almost nonexistent and my BFF appreciated my efforts. Eventually, what began to happen is I enjoyed writing those long messages (as an example). What started as me obeying the instructions of the Holy Spirit for the sake of our friendship turned into a total shift in my thinking, and my actions soon followed. I honestly do not think that God would have brought me John, when He did, had I not passed this test. It's not because He didn't want to or even planned to. It is because I would have ruined it with my mindset and my inability to love him well. Remember I said God isn't just interested in you getting married. He is interested in you having a marriage that stands the test of time. No marriage can last when individuals in the marriage are not willing to compromise and put the other before themself.

I now realize that God was teaching me what real love actually is. Love is not what society, media, or your favorite romantic comedy has taught you. It is not your marriage goals or even a feeling that you get. Love is clearly defined in 1 Corinthians 13:4-7. It is patient, it is kind, it is not jealous or boastful or proud or rude. It does not demand its own way. It is not irritable, and it keeps no record of being wronged. It does not rejoice about injustice but rejoices whenever the truth wins out. Love never gives up, never loses faith, is always hopeful, and endures through every circumstance. That is how we are called to love people, and guess what? It is not dependent on the actions of the other person. Real love is a choice. It is a choice that you make day after day, hour after hour, minute after minute, and it behaves this way irrespective of how the other person is treating us. THAT is real love. Now I can say with everything in me that I LOVE MY HUSBAND. My husband is a great person, an incredible partner, and a fantastic father, but I can honestly say that I do not love him because of those things or any of his other wonderful attributes. I appreciate those things of course, but my love is not dependent upon them, and it is not based on my emotions. My love runs so much deeper than that. I use the Word of God as a mirror to my love to make sure it is measuring up to God's standards. Until you are ready to love someone like that, you should not even bother being found because you will end up ruining what could have been a good situation had you truly been ready.

Allowing yourself to love

One day I decided that I was going to do things a little differently in my relationships. I had just begun a relationship with a guy that I liked, and I could see us going places. I had also been allowing God to heal some areas of my life that had been previously closed off. All of these factors allowed me to make a big decision. I decided that I was going to go into this relationship no holds barred. In other words, I was not going to put up any walls or hold anything back when it came to allowing myself to love this particular person. I realized this was risky because at any moment, I could get my heart broken potentially shattering my trust in that person and other relationships down the line. However, I knew that for me to truly know if this could work, I had to put everything on the line and give it my all. I owed it to myself to give all of myself in a relationship. I owed it to myself to give all of myself in a relationship. I know that sounds precarious because of the potential to be used and abused, but if we do not do this we will be doing ourselves, the other person, and the relationship as a whole a disservice.

After less than 3 months of seriously dating, the relationship ended with this guy breaking up with me. It was the first time anyone had broken up with me, and I was crushed because I loved this guy and could see us potentially getting married. I was indeed heartbroken, and it took some time to recover from that heartbreak. I had two choices, however. I could put all of my walls back up and let that experience define what the rest of my relationships would look like by becoming bitter, pessimistic, and jaded. Or I could decide to not let the actions of another human being determine how I would approach all of my other relationships. I knew that my real husband was out there somewhere, and it was only fair that I give him a fair chance and withhold no parts of me.

We cannot allow another human being to dictate how we treat others. We have to make up in our minds that we are responsible for our happiness, and we will not let the poor actions of someone in our past dictate our future. The truth is, one still has power over you if they can bring you to the point of callousness and no human being should have that type of influence over your life. I want you to decide right now that you will be confident in who you are and how God created you. If any human being fails to recognize that (and some will), it's their loss. Continue to move forward into your destiny anyhow.

It saddens me when I encounter someone who no longer believes in love or they are beginning to question the legitimacy of relationships and marriage. Some are taking a "why even bother" mentality and turning into self-professed "savages" only as a defense mechanism. Attempting to mask the pain and disappointment of failed relationships. The truth is, just because you've had relationships that have failed in the past (even if there were many) and just because you haven't had any men to prove your doubts wrong and just because you have seen other relationships and marriages fail, does not mean it does not work. It also does not mean that you are not capable of having a successful relationship yourself. Perhaps the issue is that you are looking in the wrong places, giving your heart to the wrong people, or going about it all the wrong way.

Let's imagine you have just purchased a new gadget, and you have been trying to get it to work for weeks, but it seems to be broken. Let's imagine you bought the gadget for a specific reason, but it is not doing what you need it to do. Finally, you tell yourself you're going to give up because it just does not work, and you want your money back. Here is the kicker, the issue is not with the gadget, it's you. The gadget works perfectly fine. In fact, there are no defects, it has been programmed correctly, and it is waiting to fulfill its intended purpose. You just need to pick up the user manual and figure out how to work it instead of trying to figure it out by yourself through trial and error or by asking your friend who has the same product believing they must know how to work it. Do you catch my drift? If there is anyone who knows how the gadget works, it's the manufacturer. They created the very thing you are trying to use so, it would behoove you to pick up the instructions that they meticulously took the time to write so that you could make yours work successfully for your life and needs.

Hopefully, I didn't lose you. That gadget in our imaginary example is a representation of marriage. God is the one who created relationships and marriage; it was His idea. Therefore, if you want to know its origin, its purpose, how it works, and how to have a successful one yourself, then you are going to have to take your cues from the Book that talks all about it, the Bible. If you are constantly looking to the world for its standards, its examples, and its way of doing things, then you are going to get the world's results. You will constantly find yourself falling short and living with disappointment. If you want a happy relationship and ultimately a happy marriage with a loyal man then that is available for you, however, you must be willing to abandon everything you think you know about it and everything that you have been conditioned to think about. Then, renew your mind to the right way, God's way.

If you see glimpses of yourself in any of the previous scenarios in this chapter, it is ok. We must first experience God's love to give the right type of love, to open ourselves up to love and to have the right view of love. Seek Him, be honest with Him and then let Him heal you and teach you. Make the necessary adjustments He will give you by His Spirit. Learn to love God with all your heart, your might, and your strength; everything else will flow from that relationship. Then learn to cultivate the relationships of those people He has already given you. If you do this, you will set yourself up for success in marriage, and in every relationship in your life.

Are You Ready for a Relationship?

The best thing you can do is pray and seek God where your love life is concerned. There is no one method that is one size fits all. For some, He may give peace to date people right now. For others, He may tell you not to date at all, and He will bring the right person to you. The key is to be open to His leading in every area of your life. Proverbs 3:5-6 says "Trust in the Lord with all your heart, and lean not on your own understanding; In all your ways acknowledge Him, And He shall direct your paths." That is such a beautiful promise. Sometimes we don't understand why God tells us to break it off with a specific person even when they look good on paper. We may not understand when He tells us to stop dating for a season. Sometimes we don't get it when it seems everyone else is in a relationship except us. But this scripture tells us first of all to trust Him. Then it promises that if we acknowledge Him in ALL of our ways (meaning we include Him in our decisions and ask for His direction and wisdom concerning these areas) then He will direct us. And if we have the King of Kings directing us well then we can't go wrong now, can we?

Now that I have gotten that sort of disclaimer out of the way, I want to share with you some concrete things for you to think about that may signal if you're ready for a relationship and all that comes with one. Use it as a guide to aid you in your process. The truth is, there are many people, both men and women, who are playing Russian Roulette with their love life. They're trying a little bit of this and a little bit of that only for it to eventually end in disaster. Not everyone is ready, equipped, and fully capable of being in a mature, lasting relationship. Most people just jump at the prospect of being in a relationship because they like the way it will make them feel, and they seldom stop to think about all that comes along with it. "To everything, there is a season, A time for every purpose under heaven" according to Ecclesiastes 3:1. Doing anything out of season puts you at risk for negative results. The purpose of dating, courting, romantic relationships, and the like is to eventually lead to marriage. If marriage is not the goal, then what's the point? There is nowhere in my Bible that mentions the term boyfriend/girlfriend, yet we seem to live in the day and time of the forever girlfriend or forever boyfriend. This should not be so. When you renew your mind to keep the whole purpose of dating/courting in perspective, I promise your relationships will begin to look a lot different. You will not settle for just anyone at any time. You will not tolerate any old thing. You will refuse to treat people any kind of way. Your mind will be set on forever. It will be set on your future, your legacy, a lifetime. So with that bigger picture in mind, let's explore some of the things that signal you are ready for a relationship.

1. **You are over any and all heartbreak from your past.**

   It is so easy to want to jump right into another situation after a breakup. Sometimes it's to make the other person jealous. Or it can be because we need a rebound. Occasionally, it's to keep us busy. Other times, it's a little bit of all three. Whatever the reason, it is not wise to jump right out of one relationship into another. Before you know it, you will look up and realize that you are still harboring old feelings, emotions, and issues from old connections that you did not even realize were there. It is important to take some time to pause, reflect, figure out what you could have done better, what you want, don't want, and in many cases to just heal. What you absolutely do not want to do is bring old relationship baggage into a new relationship. It is a recipe for drama and trust me, men do not like drama. It is one of the quickest ways to turn them all the way off. Furthermore, If you do not take the time to heal, you may end up projecting some of your fears and insecurities onto your new mate and end up ruining a possibly good thing.

   I had to learn this fast. Because I was used to being let down by people, I did not like it when people would tell me that we were going to do something or go somewhere and not keep their word. So when John and I were dating, I felt that familiar feeling begin to rise up in me whenever he had to change or cancel even the smallest of plans. I had to understand that sometimes people have genuine reasons for not being able to follow through. As long as it was not a consistent occurrence or a pattern, then I needed to extend him some grace. If I decided to take this personally, I would be mixing up character flaws with situational circumstances.

As I've stated before, It is important to not let your past dictate how you're going to move forward with people in the future. It is okay to be cautious, but not unreasonable. Unless you take time to really get healed and bring old issues out of the dark into light, they will always come back to haunt you. Decide that you will no longer be bound. You owe it to yourself to be free. You deserve to be free.

2. **You don't necessarily "need" a relationship and you do not need a man to complete you.**

   Desperation is never a good look, and men can usually sense it right away. But even more than that, anything that you need or develop an inordinate desire for becomes your god. Many people are coveting relationships and marriage and the truth is that is idolatry. You will know you have made marriage, a relationship, a person, or anything your idol when it consumes your thoughts, when you put it before your relationship with God, or when you compromise to get or keep it. What happens when you make anything an idol is that thing becomes your god. Of course, we would never admit it or even think that way, but that is exactly what occurs. Then when you do get a mate that person and relationship becomes your god, and it begins to make or break you. When it's going well you're happy. When it's on the rocks, your life is in shambles and you can barely function. Nothing except the only true and living God should hold that type of weight and influence in your life.

Idolatry is a sin. God makes that clear in Exodus 20:3 stating, "You shall have no other gods before me." Learn to grow in love with yourself, your God, and the people around you so that every other relationship will flow from that.

3. **You have healthy relationships with family/friends.**

This is important because the way you conduct your relationships with family, friends, and other people is a great indication of how you will operate in a romantic relationship. In our heads, we like to think that we will treat our mate better because we will be oh so in love, but feelings are fickle. Therefore, your actions need to be rooted and grounded in something other than fickle feelings and erratic emotions. They need to be grounded in love, and I am not talking about the type of love that you see on your favorite romantic comedy or hear about in your favorite R&B song. I am talking about the type of love we discussed earlier in this chapter. The agape love that God expects us to walk in every single day. That type of love is patient, kind, unconditional, forgives easily, and a host of other things as outlined in 1 Corinthians 13:4-8.

Do you still have a hard time forgiving friends or communicating effectively with family? Do you just brush things under the rug instead of addressing issues head-on? Do you lack empathy or only like to see things your way? Are you quick to listen and slow to anger? (James 1:19) All of these things take maturity, discipline, and selflessness, and all of them are needed to have a healthy, sustainable relationship and marriage. The hard truth is, if you're not walking in them yet then you're probably not ready to be in anybody's relationship. Sure you can learn as you go, but your marriage should not be burdened by things you could have mastered while you were single.

4. **You already are or you are diligently working on becoming the type of person you want to marry.**

It is so easy to have a long list of things you would like in a mate. Yet, rarely do we stop to think about what we have to offer the other person in a relationship. Have you ever stopped to ask yourself, "Am I all of those things that I am asking of a future spouse?"

Think about your "list" for a second. As you go through your mental checklist, one by one ask yourself if you possess whatever "it" is. For example, I want my husband to have good credit. Well, do you have good credit? I want my man to be in shape. Are you in shape? I want my man to be strong in the Word. Are you strong in the Word? I want my man to pray every morning before he gets his day started. Do you pray every morning before you start your day? Do you see where I am going here? It is unfair for us to demand something from someone else that we are not yet walking in ourselves. While no one expects you to be perfect, you should be making strides towards your goals, and have produced some fruit before thinking about jumping into a relationship. Matthew 7:16 says "you will know them by their fruit." This is an indication that our life will produce whatever we have been consistently sowing. Make sure you are sowing well into your future self.

5. **Your relationship with God is solid.**

This one may be last, but it is certainly not least. In fact, this is the most important thing to check off of your list. If you have this one in order, then everything else will fall into place. A solid foundation is needed for any marriage, and for believers, I would hope that foundation is Christ. He should be the center because a 3 cord strand is not easily broken (Ecclesiastes 4:12). I honestly do not know how people do it without Jesus. I call on Jesus for my marriage (and everything else) almost every day.

To have a relationship and eventually a marriage that is built on the foundation of God, your personal relationship with God needs to be solid. You have to know how to get a prayer through. You have to know who you are in Him and let Him give you your identity and your purpose. You need to build up intimacy with Him. You need to understand how much He loves you so that anyone else's love is just extra. You need to develop your faith so that when the storms of life come you can be an anchor and not a burden to your family. You need to let God develop the fruit of the Spirit in you such as charity, longsuffering, joy, peace, faithfulness, kindness, and self-control so that you can operate effectively in all of your relationships and life in general. All of this responsibility is on you to cultivate (with God's help and grace of course). It is simply not wise to try to develop a relationship with another human being until you have developed the most important relationship you will ever have, the one with your Heavenly Father, Lord & Savior, and Helper. He longs for a relationship with you.

Can you check off everything from this list? If yes, great! Continue reading for more wisdom for your next level. If your answer is no, that's ok. One of the purposes of this book is to help you get to a place where you are ready. Keep reading and journeying with me for more insight.

CHAPTER 2

Why Am I Still Single?

This is a million-dollar question for some. It is the one question that women all over the world are asking themselves. And they're also asking God, and relationship gurus, and self-help books. And if they are not asking the question then people are asking them, "Why are you STILL single?" And maybe the most annoying of all is when someone tries to come and diagnose your singleness after looking at bits and pieces of the puzzle that is your entire life. They come and offer unsolicited advice as to why you may still be unmarried. The truth is, no one can tell you specifically why you are still single, so I am not going to attempt to do that either. Instead, I am going to share my story and offer you relevant, God-inspired suggestions that I believe will help you navigate this time. If any of them confirms something in your spirit then I would encourage you to pray about that area, and let God speak to your heart with more clarity and specificity.

God's Timing

One of the most straightforward reasons why you may not be married just yet is because it is simply not the right time. There is a phrase in the Bible that I love; it is the phrase "fullness of time." Here it is in Galatians 4:4 KJV: *"But when the fulness of the time was come, God sent forth His Son, made of a woman, made under the law, To redeem them that were under the law, that we might receive adoption as sons" (Galatians 4:4-5).* I love it because it implies that God had that moment in time planned before the foundation of the world. In other words, there was a specific, inevitable point when He knew He would send His Son, and until it was that time, He was not going to send Him. However, when it was that time, nothing could stop it because the fullness of time had come. I believe that every one of us has a "fullness of time" when it comes to certain things in our lives. I believe that there are designated moments in time when specific milestones and events will be realized, and only God knows when that is.

The hard part is waiting patiently for that time to come. This is where contentment comes into play. If you are anything like I used to be then you probably loathe the word contentment. Whenever I heard the word what automatically came to my mind was "settling for what you have right now until life gets better." But that is far from the truth. Contentment is a state of happiness and satisfaction. Think about that. When you are content you are satisfied with the way your life is right now just as it is. I know what you're thinking. "But I'm not REALLY satisfied with my life just the way it is." I know because I was there. I thought I needed a relationship status, a certain amount of money in the bank, little to no conflict in my life, a certain number of friends, and a host of other things to make me feel happy, satisfied and you guessed it, content. I found out fairly quickly though that none of those things have any bearing on my contentment. Before I was in a relationship, I used to say things like, "Everybody is talking about marriage. God, I would be happy if you just brought me a mate. I want someone to have fun with, go out with, someone to love, etc."

Then John and I began courting and after a while, I began to think "Gosh, when am I going to get a ring?" Then we got engaged and I couldn't stop looking at the app on my phone counting down the days until we got married.

When I was unemployed and stayed home all day, the boredom was stifling. Then I got a job, and it kept me super busy so I found myself constantly complaining. I used to ask God for the ability to travel for work, and He graciously granted me that desire. Eventually, I found myself rolling my eyes every time I was scheduled to be away. Do you see the trend? We get all happy and excited when God blesses us or when something good happens in our lives until after a while our hearts become discontent again looking for the next "thing". The next big event, the next level, the next milestone, the next promotion. It's all about the new, now, and next. We must learn to be content with our portion, in our season, at all times. I like to put this in perspective by thinking about where God has brought me from. It makes it easier to appreciate all that I have now and fills me with a sense of gratitude. The truth is, only an authentic relationship with God can bring you the feeling of satisfaction and contentment your entire being is thirsting for. Everything else will become extra from there. Rely on God and His perfect timing for everything to come to pass in your life.

You're being hidden

I know all about being hidden. I used to think that I was unattractive or just plain invisible to the opposite sex during a certain season of my life. Nobody was checking for me. My phone was dry. No one asked me out. I couldn't even get a look from a stranger. These things ate away at my confidence to a certain extent because even though I didn't necessarily want to date anyone at the time, it still would have felt good to feel wanted. But then I realized that God was hiding me for a purpose.

Have you ever been to a jewelry store and noticed the setup? The cheap stuff that's of little to no value made with fake stones and metals are usually outside of the glass case. You can get a close look at it without having to ask anyone, and you can even touch it if you'd like. Then there's the jewelry under the glass case. This is where all the jewelry made of precious metals and stones are kept. You can't touch it or take a good look at it unless an attendant opens the case, usually with a key. But did you know there's a 3rd option? There's a place in the back that not many people are aware of. You have to KNOW that it is there to even ask about it, and there is a different protocol that must take place before you can even see it. What is the difference between all these pieces of jewelry? The level of ACCESS was different depending on the VALUE of the item. Not everyone should have access to your time, your space, and everything that is YOU. The more value you place on yourself, the more you will realize that the man who wants your heart should have to go through different protocols to even get to you. And he only knows you're there because He has sought the heart of the Father to find you.

When I began to understand that I was like that jewelry locked in the vault in the back of the store out of plain view, I began to have a different perspective of being hidden. I felt precious to God. I felt honored, cherished, and valuable. I also realized, though, that it's not every day that you get people walking in to see the stuff that's locked in the vault. So I understood that my love story might take a little more time to unfold than everyone else's around me. I understood that while I may not have been getting a lot of action in the realm of dating, in the end it was going to be well worth the wait.

When I began to understand that being hidden was actually an honor and that it was actually for my protection, I stopped fighting the process. I gladly wore God's divine veil with a godly pride knowing that one day the right man would tear right through it. He would be able to see me for who I was, his rib. My wedding day was the perfect picture of that. It may be a little old school, but I wore a long veil with the front part covering my entire face. I wore it for the entire ceremony up until John and I were pronounced husband and wife. It was at that time that my husband removed the veil and kissed me as we became one. It was a beautiful sight to see in the natural. But when I think about the removing of the veil that he did in the spirit, my heart leaps with even more felicity.

He's Not Ready

Would you ever go to a Lexus dealership to shop for a new car knowing your lifestyle could only afford a Honda? (There is nothing wrong with Hondas by the way. They are very good cars). The point is though, you would not even tease yourself by going to a place that was out of your price range because you know that eventually, the decision will come back to haunt you when you cannot afford the payments. Likewise, some men will not marry you or even attempt to get to know you because they know that they are not in a position to afford you right now. Meaning, they have some things that they may want to get together spiritually, financially, emotionally, or otherwise. I had guys tell me after the fact that they knew they couldn't approach me because they knew they had to come correct or risk messing up their chances. See, not everyone is rejecting you. Some people just have sense enough and care enough to approach you in the right way, in the right mindset, and under the right circumstances. That is the type of man you want to get yourself involved with when he does have his affairs in order.

The reality is that sometimes our man of God needs a little more time to marinate in God's presence than we do. Just like God caused Adam to fall into a deep sleep, sometimes our Adam isn't quite woken just yet. And that's okay because what you do not want is to prematurely jump into a relationship with someone who is not completely done or finished their maturation process. God knows the things He wants to work out in a person and all the things He wants to do in their hearts. It would be unwise for us to intervene with what He is doing. Doing so could distract the person and cause it to take more time for his maturation. And if you do end up in a relationship with them too soon, it could cause the relationship to end in disappointment. God's rejection is sometimes our protection so we must learn to embrace the no's and the not yet's, with just as much enthusiasm as we do the yes's.

You're Not Ready

It takes a mature person to realize, understand, and acknowledge when they are not yet ready to be married. And if you are not ready to be married, then why dive into a relationship? After all, the point of getting into a relationship is to eventually lead to marriage. Realistically, you will never be completely ready. However, God knows exactly what you need and what areas you should be developed in to present you to the person that He has for you. If we receive things too soon, what was designed to be a blessing could feel like a curse.

You would never let your 10-year-old drive a car would you? Even if you had a car prepared for their 16th birthday and you were excited to give it to them, you would still refrain from giving it to them until they were ready to drive it because you know it is for their protection. The car would do them more harm than good because they did not yet develop the skills needed to properly drive the car. Well, it is the same way with God. He will never give us anything until He knows that we are ready for it.

When I refer to not being ready, I am not referring to some tangible outward manifestation such as having good credit, looking a certain way, having a stable job, or anything like that. Instead, I am referring to a particular attitude and mindset. I am referring to a heart posture. I am referring to things that cannot be easily discerned by someone looking only at outward appearance. The truth is, many of our behavior and outward manifestations begin from those areas within first.

They say hindsight is 20/20 and that could not be more true in my case. Looking back, as I take a journey through my mind of all the Mr. Wrong's I had to go through to get to Mr. Right, I realize some of the areas I could have adjusted. It is as if, being on the other side I am looking through a completely different lens. The way I view love, relationships, men and marriage has changed drastically, and I only wish I knew then what I know now. Allow me to share some of the lessons I learned when I was not ready in hopes that you shave off some time waiting to walk into your best. You may see yourself in some of these, or none at all, but I guarantee if you pray and look introspectively, you will realize that some areas could use adjusting within you as well.

Valuable Lessons Learned

Lesson #1
I was a fixer

I was a fixer...and aren't we all? We, as in women, that is. We often take on men who are "projects" thinking we can fix them, help them, or change them. That is because we were built that way. We were designed to be HELP-meets according to Genesis 2:18. However, we were never designed to do renovations, and we surely were not designed to do all of this helping outside of the confines of marriage.

I remember all too well how I would meet someone and have an uncanny ability to see so much potential in them. I knew they were a good person who just needed a little guidance, and I thought I would be the one to help them along the way. In some cases, I even began to believe that maybe God sent them to me for that reason as if they needed me to get to where God wanted them to be. Now, looking back I can see that is just not the case. God does not call us to remain in a relationship with someone just so that we could help get him to where he needs to be spiritually or otherwise. We are not God. I had to realize that although I am a helper, I am not a fixer and I am only meant to help the man God has ordained for me.

Lesson # 2
I was attracting what I was reflecting

When I acted a certain way, dressed a certain way, and carried myself a certain way I would inevitably attract a certain caliber of men. This is because the quality of the bait will determine the quality of the catch. At one point I was not attracting ANY men at all, and I later figured out why. Like I mentioned before, men were intimidated by me because they knew they had to have certain things in order before they could even approach me. I had one guy explain to me that there are certain women who they know they want to take seriously and potentially go the long haul with BUT they have to make sure they have their stuff together so that they do not mess it up. In other words, he had to come correct.

Whether you want to believe it or not, you are giving off some sort of aura about yourself through the things you post on social media, the way you dress, the company you keep, and a whole myriad of factors. Based on those things, you will attract either your heart's desire or your worst nightmare. This is something I had to learn and make some adjustments along the way, but the results are worth it.

Lesson # 3
I didn't understand my worth

Sure I pranced around like I was God's gift, but I didn't genuinely know who I was, and I didn't truly know my value as I do now. Let me ask you a question. If a stranger were to come up to you and ask "who are you?" What would you say? Normally, we would answer with our occupation or a title of some sort such as mommy or wife. Whatever we lead with is often how we define ourselves and it is usually where we either consciously or subconsciously receive our worth from. The issue with that is, what if you were stripped of all of your titles, degrees, your occupation? What if that relationship ended? Would you still be confident in who [insert your name] is? I have seen many people crumble and not even know who they were anymore with the loss of a job or a relationship because their entire IDENTITY was wrapped up in that person or thing. At one point God stripped me of everything I put my value in so that I could see that my worth is in Him and Him alone, only then was He able to rebuild and place me on a solid foundation. Now, I know who Rita is apart from everything else, but I could not begin to even think about being anyone's wife until I got that straight.

Lesson # 4

I put up with way more than I should have for way longer than I should have

I think this is something we can all relate to, but it doesn't tend to hit us until we are out of the situation and we're like "How and why did I ever put up with all of THAT?" The same things that we would be quick to call another woman "foolish" over. Again, hindsight is 20/20 and when you are right there in the middle, it is hard to see everything that is going on. It is hard to recognize when you are being mistreated, undervalued, taken for granted, constantly let down, and everything else that you know you do not deserve. You do everything you can to rationalize or just cope for the time being because you are too comfortable to end it. Change is hard, and many times we'd rather stay in a less than appealing situation rather than muster up the courage and build enough patience to wait for our true heart's desire. But let me tell you, doing this only delays the destination. I spent many years keeping a space filled with people who did not belong there. It was a space reserved only for the right person, and God could not bring the right person until that space was completely empty. When I completely emptied that space, at a time when I was least expecting it, the love of my life presented himself.

Lesson #5
My relationship status didn't level up until I leveled up

I didn't begin to level up in any other area until I leveled up spiritually. As soon as I began to take my relationship with God seriously and make Him a priority, everything started changing in my life for the better. Relationships with family and friends improved, finances improved, heck even my looks began to improve. Every single place in my life that was crooked, God began to make straight. Every single area of my life that was dry, God began to pour down the rain of heaven onto it-including my love life.

This didn't happen because God was trying to reward me for some sort of good behavior; remember it doesn't work like that. What began to happen is that the more I began to seek after Him and spend time with Him, the more He began to change me. The more I began to surrender my will for His and allowed Him to change me, the more His desires for my life became MY desires for me. The more His desires for my life became my desires for my life, the more I got on His path, and therein lies the key. Once you get on the path that God has for you, there is no reason for you not to run right into every single thing that God has for your life, including your God-given mate.

Many people have not even begun to come close to the path because they have not yet relinquished their ways, their will, and their plans in exchange for His. The reason they haven't relinquished their ways and plans for His is because they haven't been seeking Him and developing in Him as they should. The plans and promises that God has already spoken over your life are plenty and they are beautiful, but they are not automatic. If that was the case, everyone would be walking in it, but we know that is not the case. Instead, they are contingent upon you getting into alignment with the will of God for your life.

Little by little, but very deliberately, God began to upgrade me and eventually led me straight into the path of my husband, John. If you know you are already on the right path, then get excited, because as you continue to walk with the Lord His desires become your desires and He promises that as we delight ourselves in Him, He gives us the desires of our hearts (Psalm 37:4). However, if you know you have veered off of the path then decide today that you are going to get back on. God longs to meet you in the secret place and lead you into all that He has for you. He has not changed His mind about His good and perfect plans for your life.

PART II

Him

CHAPTER 3

That's Not Your Husband

You know the story. Boy meets girl. Boy asks girl for her phone number (or vice versa). Boy & girl start "talking." Boy and girl hit it off instantly, so much so that they stay on the phone late into the night getting to know one another. Sometimes it gets so late that they struggle to wake up for work or school the next morning. Days pass and they continue to talk and maybe even FaceTime. They also text; they text A LOT. They may even go on a few unofficial dates or social gatherings. Then weeks go by, maybe even months or God forbid years, and all of a sudden there is a shift- something changes. Communication wanes. The texts aren't as frequent. Girl finds herself initiating the conversations more and more. Phone calls are almost non-existent and those unofficial dates? Forget about it.

What happened? Did you do something wrong? Was it something you said? Something you didn't do? Maybe, but more often than not, it's none of the above. More than likely the change has nothing to do with your actions at all but more to do with the guy's intentions towards you. I have found that many times, the reason falls into one of these 3 categories:

Reason #1: He's not ready to be in a committed relationship

This is the guy who likes the idea of being in a relationship, but he is not yet mature enough to take on the responsibility of a relationship. He likes the perks and benefits such as companionship, someone to talk to, someone to go out and have fun with, and having the security of knowing someone is in his corner. However, this person has not yet decided to settle down. He is still more interested in being with his friends than being with a woman, and he wants to have his cake and eat it too. Stay far away from this type. Why? Because it's easy to fall for his charm and his expressed desire to be in a relationship, but his mixed signals will leave you frustrated and confused.

Reason #2: There's someone else

In this case, the guy has started talking to someone else but is afraid to tell you, or he was already talking to someone else and is now trying to "get to know" the both of you at the same time. Run far away! The man God has for you will pursue you with purpose and passion, and you will not have to compete for his time or attention. He will be decisive. You will not have to convince him. He will choose you.

Reason #3: You're not the one for him

More than likely this guy is just wasting your time until the right one comes along because although he may desire to be in a relationship, he just cannot see himself with YOU long term. You may feel tempted to feel bad about yourself at the thought of this, but please do not. Every woman is not for every man and vice versa. Rejection is no respecter of persons. It does not mean that you are not good enough or that there is something wrong with you. All it means is that you are not the right one for him, and truth be told he probably isn't the right guy for you. To the right guy, you will be EVERYTHING. You will be more than what they ever wanted or knew they needed. And don't buy the right girl, wrong timing line because again (say it with me this time) THE MAN GOD HAS FOR YOU WILL PURSUE YOU WITH PURPOSE AND PASSION. Nothing can get in his way if he truly wants you.

I have experienced each of the above previous scenarios at some point during my single life, and I have watched it play out in the lives of friends. Every time someone vents to me I want to shout from the mountaintops the same words Jesus was probably yelling at me when I was entertaining men who were not right for me: THAT'S NOT YOUR HUSBAND.

Let's Just See Where This Goes (or let's not)

"Let's just see where this goes" is a line that I am all too familiar with. Whether someone was feeding it to me or I was the one doing the feeding, the end result was never good. Let's just see where this goes is just a nice way to say: "I am not completely sold on you yet, but I want to keep you around because you're meeting some type of need for me at the moment". Even if the actual words aren't uttered, you know you're in a "let's just see where this goes" type of situationship, if it has not yet been made clear that the two of you are in an exclusive relationship or if intentions have not been clearly defined on the future of your relationship.

Sadly, "it's complicated" is many people's relationship status right now. In each situation, the beginning and middle may be a little different, but the ending always ends up the same: heartbreak. I have witnessed too many broken hearts, bruised egos, and unmet expectations simply because a conversation was never had communicating the intentions of each party in the relationship with the corresponding action. And in many cases, even if someone has made it clear with their words that they do not want a relationship, the little rendezvous continues. Let's face it, in the back of our mind we always think that we can change their mind and if we're honest, we like the attention that we're getting from them at the moment.

In the past, I have let months go by doing things with guys that would make me think we were a couple only to find out that we were "just friends". Their actions confused me into believing otherwise, and I would become increasingly frustrated. There was a point in time where I wanted to put all of the blame and responsibility on the men who I felt did me wrong and led me on. Why would they ask for my number if they had no real interest in getting to know me? Why would they ask me out on a date if they weren't feeling me? Why would they go out of their way to call and text me every day if they didn't like me? These very well may have been valid questions but the truth is this, I had to learn how to take responsibility for my own happiness and thus my heartbreaks.

No one is responsible for protecting my heart except me. Sure, you would hope that a person has your best interest in mind but ultimately it is our responsibility to be keepers of our own heart and to guard it with vigilance until we find someone worth opening it up for. Now, this does not mean being afraid to get hurt or putting a padlock on our hearts, because if we are truly free from past disappointments, emotional heartbreaks, and failed relationships, then we would freely and openly give a fair and honest opportunity to love when it does present itself. There is a difference between guarding your heart and being guarded. What it does mean, however, is that we are good stewards over our hearts by being led by the Holy Spirit in our (potential) relationships, properly vetting potential mates before getting our feelings involved, not ignoring red flags and checks in our spirit, and not settling just because we want to be in a relationship.

You know what we like to tell ourselves: "A man is supposed to lead and be the head". As a result, we trust that he would lead us both in the right direction. But the reality is if two people aren't married, nobody is the head of no one and each person is responsible for the protection of their own heart. I came to realize that I was just as much, if not more responsible, for any of the confusion and heartbreak that resulted as a consequence of me just going with the flow in those situations. I want you to understand this truth: No one can protect you except you (with the help of God of course). You owe it to yourself to be diligent in vetting possible love interests, keeping your head on straight, and not allowing someone to just string you along. You cannot expect another individual to do that for you. You cannot put that type of power and influence over your life into someone else's hands, especially someone who has not even professed devotion and real solid intentions toward you. Ultimately, a man is going to look out for his own needs especially if he is not yet invested in you.

Earlier I mentioned the mindset of some men. It is the one that says: "I'm not completely sold on you yet, but I want to keep you around because you're meeting some type of need for me right now." What type of need you ask? It's easy to automatically assume the need is sexual, but in many cases, the woman may not even have a sexual relationship with the man. Here's the thing: A lot of times it is out of the man's selfishness that he keeps women strung along because of little voids that are being filled. These voids and needs include but are not limited to:

Companionship: He needs someone to hang out with and enjoys your company.

Emotional Security: He connects with you on an emotional level and feels he can open up to you in some ways or he has some sort of attachment to you such as history, a child, or otherwise.

Ego: He likes what you do for his ego. You celebrate him. He knows he can always count on you to be there. He likes the admiration that he receives from people when he takes you out in public.

Time killer: He understands that you're always going to be there because you always make yourself available. So he texts, calls, or wants to hang out with you out of the blue most of the time when he has little or no other options. He likes to keep you in his back pocket. It's mostly a relationship out of convenience.

Sexual: You are filling some type of sexual desire even if the two of you have never even gone all the way.

Keep in mind, the void or need may also be any combination of two or more of the categories mentioned.

Until a person knows better, they cannot do any better and head knowledge is not enough. I am sure most men know in theory that doing certain things will cause a woman to get the wrong idea but they may not have gotten any real revelation on it just yet; the light bulb has not yet come on for them. Similarly, in theory, we as women know that we should not just be going with the flow without a man making his intentions clear. Yet, we go with it for some of the same reasons that the man does either because:

1. We are selfish and we too are getting some of the same needs met as the man (the only difference is most times we think he will realize what he has and lock us down).

2. We have not received a real revelation of the consequences of our actions (even if we have experienced them over and over again.).

3. We have settled for it and have come to terms that we'd rather have this than nothing at all.

So how do you avoid all of this? Well, as much as men hate it, sometimes the "What are we" conversations are necessary. If after the first few consistent encounters, he has not at least made his intentions for you clear, then it is a conversation that must be had. You will never know where you are going if someone does not say it. Does that mean that you have to rush off and get engaged the same year? Of course not, but it does mean that you don't have to go out with someone a thousand times before he at least knows whether or not he wants to date you exclusively and begin courting you. It's not rocket science. Either he does or he doesn't. We're the ones who tend to make it complicated.

Many times men are afraid that they are going to miss out on something better. Oftentimes, they are not completely sold on a particular woman just yet, and if that's the case then one must let them go. You should never have to convince someone of your worth. The right person will be able to recognize it, and he will CHOOSE you. The man God has for you will choose you out of a sea of billions of other women. Pretty women, smart women, funny women, women with careers, women that go to his church, women that live in his city, all types of women. He will look past all of them, and only see you. I know because I've experienced both sides. I know what it's like to be an option that someone just picked up when it was convenient for them, and I know what it's like to be chosen and to have a man not let any obstacle get in his way to choose me and prove it to me over and over again. You deserve to be chosen, sis. You're no one's seat filler. You're no one's option on a menu, you're the appetizer, main course, and the cherry on top of the desert. So, love yourself enough to walk away from any situation that is not headed in the direction of your true heart's desire, and make room for the person who will.

**Prophetic Word

Some of you can trust God with every other area of your life. You trust Him with your finances, your health, your purpose, your dreams, your aspirations and you've seen Him do great and mighty things in those areas, but for some reason, you will just not give Him THIS area of your life. I hear the Lord saying "My hand is not too short, my ears are not too heavy" (Isaiah 59: 1). Give this area over to me, let go of it, and surely you will say "The Lord has done great things for us and we are glad" (Psalm 126:3).

Rookie Mistakes

A few important tips you should adhere to and rookie mistakes I want you to avoid.

1. **Avoid entertaining random guys and going out on "just because" dates.**

   There are a few reasons for this. First of all, one of the most valuable resources that you have is your time and you should not be wasting it hanging out with a person you do not believe has the potential to be your future mate. You must consider, what is the end game here? If it isn't to truly get to know the person to see if you could pursue a relationship and marriage then what's the point? A free meal? A good time? We like to tell ourselves, oh well we're just friends or we're just getting to know each other to see where this goes. That is a recipe for disaster. You have to go into every [potential] relationship with purpose. You must be intentional. This is how we find ourselves compromising. We tell ourselves we will only go out to lunch with someone. We convince ourselves it will be harmless, only to find ourselves years later still "talking" to the same person. All the while we are silently frustrated because they are not living up to our expectations. However, when if we're honest, we were never supposed to even entertain the person in the first place.

Sis, date yourself! As a matter of fact, go out on a date with Jesus, I'm telling you He is the ultimate gentleman and He always foots the bill ;) You may think that's a weird concept but I used to go on dates with Jesus all the time and it was a way that I could develop my relationship with Him and get in some QT. It is a way I developed intimacy with the Lord, and learned to hear His voice. We would go to the park, restaurants, festivals, wherever. Sometimes I would take my journal and Bible, and other times I didn't. Make it fun. The Bible says that your Maker is your husband (Isaiah 54:5). Cling to God more than you cling to the desire to be in a relationship or have some sort of male companionship. He will set the bar high for any male who tries to court you. He will help raise your standards.

2. **Do not jump into a relationship fresh off the altar (and don't jump into a relationship with someone fresh off the altar).**

    I remember shortly after I got saved before my mind was renewed to certain things, I decided to try an online dating app. Go ahead, judge me. Anyhow, by this time I had already decided that I was saving my body for my future husband by abstaining from sex until marriage. Consequently, I felt it was important to let him know this pretty early on to set expectations and not waste either of our time. So during our second date after a wonderful evening at an amazing restaurant topped off with good conversation, I decided it was a good time to bring up the subject. Apparently, I was mistaken though because homeboy ripped into me and proceeded to tell me how many women have tried to play this game with him in the past. Furthermore, he didn't believe that I was saving myself. Instead, he insisted I was attempting to use and manipulate him. It went from being a perfectly beautiful evening to an awkward mess. That was the longest drive home ever.

    So, I had a decision to make. I could continue going out with him after hearing his response to something that I was indeed serious about and not willing to compromise on just to "see where things would go from there". I could also just continue to go out with him for the free meals, good conversation, and a good time, or I could cut it off right then and there knowing that it was the right thing to do. So that night, I decided in my heart that I was not going to date just for the sake of dating. Rather, I would date with intention. Now this was not my 1-year dating hiatus just yet. However, I had decided that I was going to take some time to just focus on growing my relationship with God and cultivating that part of my life. I was no longer going to seek out a relationship or try to make myself seen.

I think it is so very important to take the time to be intentional and grow in your relationship with God without the distraction (for lack of a better word) of a mate or potential mate. After all, it is a relationship and relationships take WORK! If you are at the beginning stage of a relationship, it is hard to focus on anything else. Think about when you're all in love especially in those beginning stages. All you want to do is talk to or be with that person. It is hard to eat, sleep, or do anything else besides think about them or be with them. Likewise, if you are trying to grow in your relationship with God while at the same time pursuing a romantic relationship, more than likely someone is going to get the short end of the stick. You are going to neglect one of those relationships and more than likely it is going to be the one with God. I have witnessed countless individuals who started out on fire for God, but prematurely jumped into a relationship, ended up getting hurt, and let all of their fire burn out.

This ought not to be so! Ecclesiastes 3:1 says to everything there is a season. If you seek God FIRST I truly believe that everything else will be added unto you according to Matthew 6:33. This is how I have purposed to live my life and God has truly honored it. You are going to need the solid foundation of a strong relationship with God for every single thing He is going to add unto you. Make sure you are taking the necessary steps now so that later on everything you have will not crumble.

3. **Do not jump into a relationship fresh out of a breakup.**

This one should be obvious, but I see people do it all the time so I thought I would mention it. After a breakup you need time to heal; it's just not wise to jump from one relationship into the next. It does not matter if the breakup was your idea or the other person's choice. It does not matter if there was sex involved or not. It doesn't even matter if you all were in an actual relationship or just getting to know one another. There always needs to be some sort of healing and reflection that takes place to not carry the same baggage, dysfunction, and wrong thinking and actions into the next relationship. Getting a rebound is a terrible idea. Another person will not solve your issues. You must be brave enough to be alone sometimes and mature enough to learn from previous mistakes you may have made in your past relationships. Do not rush or step ahead of God. Otherwise, you will find yourself going around the same proverbial mountain.

Be okay with saying, "that's not my husband". And be brave enough and settled enough, to wait until the real thing presents himself.

C H A P T E R   4

The One

Is there really such a thing as the One?

The term "the One" has been thrown around a lot, especially in Christian circles. There is this notion that there is this one specific person who God has designed for just one other specific person. Some people may even refer to this person as a soulmate. Whatever you want to label it, this notion is one that I have gone back and forth on for as long as I can remember. So, I would like to flush out my thoughts on the subject once and for all right here, right now.

As you know, God has given us free will, and He does not force anything on us. Instead, He allows us to make the necessary decisions for our lives, including who we should marry. With that being said, just because God does not impose His will upon us, that does not mean that every decision is the right decision. After all, He allows us to choose or not choose Him, and we all know what the right decision is in that case. He also allows us to choose our career, but that does not negate the fact that He put us here for a specific purpose and that we should seek to pursue that purpose for our life above all. I could go on and on about what God allows us to do, but I think it is safe to say that some choices are more expedient than others.

Shortly after I rededicated my life to God, I remember a significant encounter I had with the Lord. I was alone in my apartment, and I had recently received the Baptism of the Holy Spirit with the Bible evidence of speaking in other tongues. At this time, I was praying in the Spirit when suddenly, a song began to rise up in my spirit. I began to sing the words to the song out loud. The song was "Yes" by Shekinah Glory. The crazy part is back then I was not familiar with this song. I certainly did not know all of the lyrics. Nevertheless, the words began to pour out of me. As I continued to sing, I got the impression that there was something huge that God was about to ask of me, and He wanted to know if I would tell Him "yes". God was not telling me exactly what "it" was, though. He just wanted me to give Him my "yes" before He even revealed what He wanted me to do. So, there I was: kneeling down, face to the floor as tears flowed onto the carpet and snot poured out of my nose, unabashedly and emphatically saying yes to God no matter what it was He was asking of me. I left that living room completely changed. Something was different. I just couldn't put my finger on exactly what it was. I promise I am going somewhere with this. I will circle back to the One in a second, so stick with me.

Several months went by before I discovered what I was saying yes to. When it came, I was in complete shock. What God was asking of me would change my life as I knew it. What exactly did He tell me to do? The Lord told me to leave law school right after I had just completed my first year of Law School. You must understand that I had aspirations of becoming a defense attorney. I was doing well in all of my classes. I was set to be on the mock trial team the following year. I was in the middle of an internship with the Rockdale County Public Defender's Office. Not to mention financial aid was my only source of income at the time. It was a tall order and a hard decision to make, but after asking for many confirmations and waiting until the very last minute, I did it. I withdrew myself from law school and followed through on the "yes" I had given God just a few months prior when I did not know exactly what I was saying yes to.

It has been 8 years since that yes, and I have come to discover an important truth. That experience in my living room was not just about saying yes to leaving law school. I now realize that the way I live my life poured out to God, is a continual yes to Him. What I did that day was not simply telling Him yes for that one time on that one occasion. The reason I felt so changed is that I had given God a lifetime yes. I was saying, "God I will choose your will over my own every. single. time. I will lay down the plans and goals and hopes that I had for my life and instead take up the ones you have for me. I will not add you to the life that I already have. Instead, I will surrender my life to you, offer it as a living sacrifice, and allow you to transform it no matter what that looks like".

Whew, that is some heavy stuff. I came to that realization after facing many decisions in life when I wanted to go one way, but I could just feel a heavy tug to go in a different direction or make the decision that did not seem the most logical. Over and over again though, I have witnessed God's plan for my life unfold so beautifully that I could have never come up with this stuff for myself even if I had the most detailed 5, 10, or 20-year plan.

I had to give you that backdrop so that you could understand my rationale regarding "the one". When it was time for me to make a decision concerning my love life, it was no different. I had always believed and trusted that God would send me the man that He saw fit for me. Without knowing all the details, I just knew that this man, whoever he was -would be perfect...for me. My prayer for my husband at some point when I was single became something like this: "God, I pray for the husband you have for me. I pray that whoever he is, he loves you more than any and everything, including me, and that He is growing in His relationship with you daily. I pray that you are blessing the work of his hands and causing everything that he does to prosper. God, I pray that when we find each other, we will know it and there will be no doubt in either of us that we have found 'the one'". Consequently, because I was praying that way, I had an expectation that God would bring my husband to me in His perfect timing. I also always allowed God into my dating life and made space for Him there because He was "the one" I was expecting to make it happen. This looked like checking in with Him before I went on dates, honoring that feeling when I didn't have peace about a guy, and taking some time to not date at all when I felt led to go into a season of relationship fasting.

Even though I was praying that way, I was still completely taken aback when it began to unfold the way I prayed, but not at all with whom I would have ever imagined. The way my husband and I got together is one of the most supernatural things I have ever experienced. We attended the same church and considered ourselves friends since we hung in some of the same circles and attended the same small group. About 2 years after knowing each other as just friends, the Lord began speaking to us concerning one another (separately). He let John know that I was his wife and He let me know that John was my husband. Although this was happening around the same time for both of us, we did not know it at the time. We tried to work through the shock by ourselves while trying to process what we believed we were hearing from God since back then, neither one of us had any sort of interest in the other.

God explicitly told me that I was not supposed to share what I knew with John. I guess He just gave me the revelation to prepare me so that I wouldn't think John was crazy when he approached me. I did not know how God was going to make this happen or when, I just sat back and trusted that He would. Sure enough, just 3 days after asking God for confirmation, I received a series of texts from John and then a phone call and then some more texts where he finally mustered up enough courage to tell me what the Lord was saying to him. I am sure my response shocked him because when he told me via text that I'm his wife. All I said was "I know" and the rest is history. We were engaged after 9 months of courting and were married on a beautiful Fall Sunday in October of 2015.

John later explained the way God presented me to him, and I believe it could put an end to this whole "the One" debate, but I will let you draw your own conclusion. God did not force me onto John and say "Here, this is your wife. Marry her or else." Instead, it was just that, a presentation, similar to how God presented Eve in the Garden of Eden. God woke Adam up, presented Eve to him and waited to see what Adam would call her. Then Adam said, "This is now bone of my bones, and flesh of my flesh. She shall be called woman, for she was taken out of man." (Genesis 2:23). God opened John's eyes to me and essentially said "this is my best that I have for you." I may not be the best for any other man. But for John, I am His best. God let John know that he could continue down the path he was already on with another woman (which was not a bad choice, it was just not God's choice) or he could CHOOSE the woman He was presenting (me) which would lead to complete fulfillment of everything God had for him.

Everyone's story is different, and it will not happen this way for everyone, but the idea is the same. God lets us choose whomever we want, but not every good decision is a God decision. I don't know about you, but I want God's best for my life, including and especially when it comes to the person I marry. That one decision will affect your life forever, and it has the ability to shift the entire course of your life since there are so many things connected to who you marry.

Now, John and I are living in the fruit of what it means to be married to God's best. God knows exactly what we need, and He even knows those secret desires in our hearts that we have not even articulated. I cannot tell you how many times I have laughed silently to myself after witnessing something occur in our union that I have never even uttered to a soul but was such a weighty personal desire for me. So, the term, "the One", soulmate, purpose mate, or whatever you want to call it is not all that important. What I know to be true and vitally important is that it pays to let God write your love story. It pays to be open to His leading. It pays to make space for Him in your love life and dating affairs. What I know just as surely as I know my name is that I have truly found THE ONE whom my soul loves (Song of Solomon 3:4).

How I Knew He Was the One

I am often asked, "How will I know if he's the one?" Well, I hate to use the old cliche' but you will just know when it's right. Some people will know right away and for others, it may take some time, but believe me, you will know. If you have to question it, then that probably isn't it. There are different factors to consider for every person, so I do not want to tell you how you will know when you have found the one. Instead, I have decided to let you know how I knew I had found the one in the hopes that you can glean from some of the overarching themes. So, how did I know John was my husband? Well besides the fact that God told me? Let's dig in.

1. He pursued me. This was important because it seems like in this day and age there aren't many men who are actively pursuing women. Men, by nature, are hunters, but only when they find something or in this case, someone they want. There is not much that can get in the way of a man who has found someone with whom he believes he could spend the rest of his life. Many times, guys will try to make excuses for not being able to fully commit such as finances, career, debt, a busy life, or other circumstances. And while those may be valid factors, for the right person, all of those issues will become non-factors. We make time for what and who we want, and we make room for them in our life no matter what may be going on.

    Do you remember this phrase I mentioned earlier: "right girl, wrong timing?" Well, let me paint a picture for you. Have you ever had someone ask you to give them a ride somewhere and you didn't feel like doing them the favor, but you agree to do it anyway? Let's imagine, when it's time to drive them it starts raining outside a little. Then, you can't find your keys right away, so you spend some time searching and eventually find them. Then, you get in the car and realize the sound system in your car isn't working. So now you're frustrated because you have to drive in silence. You are just about ready to call your friend and let them know that you're unable to take them. Sure, the circumstances surrounding the favor are not the best, but you could still give your friend the ride if you really wanted to. It just may be a little inconvenient.

Now let's pretend the destination was a little different and you were supposed to be going to your favorite artist's concert instead. A little bit of rain doesn't seem that bad anymore does it? Sure, you misplaced your keys for a bit but at least you found them right? No music? who cares? You're on your way to all the music your heart desires. Sure, these are agitations, but you are going somewhere that you desire to go so those things now seem small to you, and you will not let it hinder you from getting what you want.

Do you see where I am going with this little hypothetical? There were situations in both of our lives at the time that would make anyone want to cower back, but John pursued me relentlessly. From day one, he made clear his intentions for me and our relationship, and he backed it up with his actions. There was no confusion, only clarity. I am not saying that the two of you have to be talking about getting married during week 1, but I am saying that you should not have to question whether or not someone is really into you and where the two of you are going after investing in one another for a certain period of time.

2. I had an abundance of peace. One of the most common ways that God leads us is through His peace or the lack of His peace in a given situation. I will expound upon this more in the next section. But for now, know that when I am in a situation and I need to hear from God, but I do not necessarily "hear" Him saying anything, I get still for a moment and wait to see if my peace is disturbed. I'm sure you've experienced this before, but you probably were not aware that you were being led by God. For example, you have plans to go somewhere but "something"

is telling you not to go because you just don't "feel" right about it even though everything on the outside seems normal. Well, that is not a "something", that is the Holy Spirit leading you and guiding you by disturbing the peace of God that is already in you if you are born again. You can sense it in your gut.

The opposite can be true as well. For example, you can be in a position where your circumstance on the outside seems crazy, but on the inside, you have such an incredible peace- that is because you are right where you are supposed to be, and the peace of God is with you. See, the Spirit knows all things and if you are born again, then that same Spirit who is the Holy Spirit of God lives on the inside of you (1 Corinthians 3:16) which means that you have access to what He knows (1 John 2:20). The problem is that many times we do not take the time to get before God to seek out those truths.

When John and I got together, it is not that the circumstances surrounding our relationship were perfect. In fact, there were several outside circumstances that would have killed other relationships, but the peace of God was so incredibly strong that I knew He was with us and that we were right where we were supposed to be. This was completely different from all of the other relationships and situationships I found myself a part of in the past. Even if the person seemed like a good fit for me, I never had any peace about any of them. It's just that I would always override it and continue talking to the person only to be heartbroken when it was all said and done. This is why I always say that you must allow the Holy Spirit to lead you and guide you in relationships because some situations can be deceiving. If you rely on outside circumstances or your own wisdom to guide you to "the one", you will be highly disappointed.

3. God would speak to me about him. Many times, I did not even have to solicit God's advice. Instead, certain situations would come up, and I would just begin to sense God speaking to me and giving me directions. For example, when John and I got into our first disagreement as a dating couple, God gave me instructions on what to do to resolve the issue. He would tell me things like - I needed to give him grace or to be more patient or to just pray for him. This was so different for me because in all of my other situationships God was completely silent unless He was telling me not to move forward with the person. It is sort of like when your mother asks you to do something, but you never do it so she's not going to tell you anything else until you do what she has already asked you to do? She is basically giving you the cold shoulder.

   I like to think that's how God is sometimes. You may have prayed about a particular person or situation, and He may not have spoken yet. That silence may be His disapproval. If you do decide to move forward, make sure you slow down to sense whether or not you have that peace we discussed earlier. So because God was speaking to me about John, I took that as His approval because why would He be giving me instructions about someone He didn't want to see me with in the first place.

4. Everything came together easily. Many external issues were occurring in my life at the time John and I began dating, so I was not exactly sure that it was even time for me to be considering marriage. For example, I wanted to be in a certain position financially before getting married, and I was not quite there yet. As a result that bothered me. There was a list of other things that I had written on a sheet of paper that I needed

God to do in my personal life for me to comfortably walk into marriage with peace of mind. Well, before John and I said "I do" every single thing was taken care of. One by one, I was able to scratch everything off of that list, and I just stood in amazement at how God had taken care of every single thing. John and I even had the wedding of our dreams and had it paid for months in advance without having to put anything on credit. When God is in the midst of a situation, He will make sure that everything works out for your good and that it happens effortlessly because His hand is on it.

Gaining a Deeper Understanding

There are questions to ask yourself and things to consider when getting involved with a potential mate. Oftentimes, a man will give away much about his character, intentions, and the condition of his heart without you even having to ask him. The Bible describes this as fruit. Matthew 7:15-16 says ""Beware of false prophets who come disguised as harmless sheep but are really vicious wolves. You can identify them by their fruit, that is, by the way they act" (NLT). A man can profess certain things with his mouth and even put up a good front for a certain amount of time, but eventually, his true nature comes out in the form of his actions. The issue is that most of the time when we run into a red flag, we like to ignore it, sweep it under the rug, or discount it. Maya Angelou was onto something when she said "When someone shows you who they are, believe them the first time." For some reason, we women like to hang around and wait for the 2nd, 3rd, 4th, or 100th time to finally decide we've had enough. That is after we've been lied to, taken for granted, let down, betrayed, and heartbroken. The same things that you may be sweeping under the rug will eventually become the same things that bring you the biggest frustrations later on - if you stick around.

Instead of going around the same mountains with guy after guy, try inspecting his fruit by keeping a lookout for the following things early on:

1. **Does he keep his word?**- When I was single, I threw my "list" in the trash after talking to God one day. I let Him know that I was no longer going to limit myself with a list and just trust that whomever he has for me, will be perfect for me. However, I did keep a few non-negotiables such as 'Must love God" and even a few suggestions such as "Can he be tall?" and yes God did oblige me. Another one of my non-negotiables was "must keep his word". It was important to me that any man I even considered dating be a man of his word. I had been let down too many times in the past by people closest to me, so I knew this was not an area I was willing to compromise on.

    Besides that, if a man can keep his word in even the smallest situations, it is an indication that he is dependable and a man of great character and integrity. He knows that his word is one of the most valuable things that he has, and it also shows the value that he places on you and your future together. Granted, sometimes people do have situations that come up beyond their control. However, if he starts off by not keeping his word, or if you notice a pattern and not just a one-off situation, then chances are he is not very dependable or he does not value YOU enough to keep his word. In any case, this is a big red flag. You deserve someone you can count on and not someone who you cannot deem as dependable.

2. **How does he treat his mother or the other women in his life?** If you want a good indication of how you will be treated by a man in the future, study the way he treats his mother or any other significant female in his life. How does he speak to her? Does he go out of his way to do nice things for her? Does he honor and cherish her? If he treats his own mother badly, the odds of him treating you any better are slim to none. The way that he treats his mother, sister or any other significant female figure indicates his level of respect as well as his attitude towards women. So pay attention to his phone conversations with her, the way he treats her at family functions, or even the way he talks about her in casual conversation. You could also ask a few questions about their relationship if it comes up in casual conversation.

   A man's relationship with his mother is a very important aspect of his behavior in relationships and could have a huge effect on them. You also want to watch out for the mama's boys and men whose mothers did a lot for them especially later in life. He may put some of those same expectations on you or it could cause some sort of strain on the relationship. Those types of things can be talked through, however. The major red flag is a man has no regard for his mother and treats her poorly. Run far away if you notice this behavior.

3. **Does he make you better?** Any man you are considering going the long haul with should help improve your life and make you a better person in some way. At the very least, he should make you *want* to be a better person. When he opens his mouth does he speak with wisdom? Are you able to discuss biblical truths with him, or are you the only one who can

discuss scripture? Does he know how to encourage you when you need it? Can he teach you new things, expose you to new experiences, or show you new places?

You want someone who is going to be able to add value to your life, not someone who sucks all of the life out of you. As women, we are natural givers and nurturers. Because this may be a place of familiarity, we have to be careful not to drain ourselves in a relationship. Pay attention to how you feel after you leave him. Are you drained or refreshed? Uplifted or cast down? Full of joy or depressed? Full of peace or uneasy?

4. **Is he good with kids?** Even if the two of you decide you do not want kids, it is still important to observe how your potential partner interacts with them. If a man is not good with kids right now, that does not necessarily mean he is a bad person or that he will never be good with kids. He just may need some developing or have not had much opportunity to be around children. However, if he is good with kids and he doesn't have any of his own just yet, that is a good sign. What this demonstrates is that he is tenderhearted and has a nurturing side among other things. If he goes out of his way to volunteer with children, if he babysits his nieces and nephews from time to time, or even if he likes holding babies whenever he gets around one, these are all good signs. Of course, if the two of you do decide to get married and have kids, he will more than likely make a great parent which is a huge asset. You have to remember that anyone you marry also has the potential to be the father of your children, so you want to make sure your guy has the potential to be a great partner in that area.

5. **How does he treat waiters/waitresses/people in public service?** If you want to see a person's true nature exposed, take them to a restaurant with horrible service and just watch and listen for their reaction. From this, you should be able to gauge their patience, see if they are easily angered, rude, or prideful.

   One of the things that I admire about my husband is that he is extremely kind and patient whenever we receive subpar service from a waiter or waitress. In fact, if the service is terrible, he usually insists that we give the person an even bigger tip than was originally intended. He says things like, "Maybe they are having a bad day" or "They could be going through something" or "Let's show them the love of Christ". Things like that in a person tend to reveal if they are a doer of the Word and not just a hearer, and it gives you a good idea of the type of person they will be even when no one is around- that is real integrity.

6. **Do your purposes align?** I hate to break it to you, but the reason why God joins two people into holy matrimony is not to make them happy. Sure, God is concerned about your happiness, and He wants to give you the desires of your heart. However, above all else, God is concerned about His purpose prevailing. "Many are the plans in a person's heart, but it is the LORD's purpose that prevails" according to Proverbs 19:21 (NIV). Therefore, God's main purpose in bringing two people together in a marriage is to carry out a bigger purpose. Every single marriage has a kingdom assignment/purpose here on the earth. This is why it is important to make sure that the assignment you are carrying aligns with the assignment on your potential husband's life. That does not mean the two

purposes must look exactly the same. However, they must complement one another in some way and must not conflict. For example, you can't have a wife who knows her purpose is to be a missionary with a husband who knows he is called to be a celebrity chef. Those two things just do not align. That type of couple will always be away from one another. When conversations begin to commence about your purposes, you should be able to see at least a glimpse of how the two of you can come together even if you do not yet see the entire picture just yet.

This is why it should be a prerequisite for both parties involved in the relationship to know what their purpose in life is. A man who does not yet know his purpose will lead you to nowhere. A wife's job is to be a helpmeet. What are you helping him with if he does not even know his assignment? There is no assignment to help him with. This will lead to much frustration in the marriage because both positions will be left unfilled. When people are operating in their divine purpose in life and in their relationship, there is little to no room left for frustration and conflict. You all don't have to know the big picture, but there must already be some level of revelation from God in this area.

Obedience is Better than Sacrifice

Do you want to know the secret sauce to fulfill the plan of God for your life? Obedience. Obedience is fueled by your total surrender to God. It's what made me say yes to God that day on my living room floor even though I had no idea what I was saying yes to. I would not be where I am today without being obedient to God in the big and the small things. In the same way, if I do not continue to be obedient to Him, I will not arrive at the destination He has already prepared for me (or at least not anytime soon).

Surely, God will never give up on you. He is full of mercy and compassion, and He is so very patient with all of us. But at the same time, we all have free will, and just like the people of Israel traveling around the wilderness, we can turn an 11-day trip into a 40-year journey if we are not careful to follow the leading and guidance of our Lord. Things that may not seem significant to you may actually be a really big deal to God. You may sense God convicting you about a certain area, but you keep brushing it off as no big deal. Meanwhile, you're crying to Him at night praying for a husband to love and cherish you. But He's looking down saying, "Daughter I can't bring him to you until you change C. But you can't change C until you do what I told you with B. But you won't even know about B until you do the first thing I told you to do, which is A." Do you catch my drift? God has a plan, and He unfolds His plan to us in pieces-little by little, step by step. But if we have yet to move on step A then we have a long way to go. I have found that it is often the small but consistent steps of obedience that lead to big promotion. Let me give you an example of this.

One day, during my season of unemployment, I heard the Lord speak to me and say "Dress for the kind of job you want". I knew I wanted a corporate job where I would be required to wear nice business clothes, so that is the type of clothes I began wearing. Keep in mind, I was completely unemployed with nowhere to go. Some days, I would go to Starbucks or a fast-food restaurant just to get out of the house and change the scenery. Trust me, it seemed pretty silly for me to walk around my house or my local McDonald's dressed like a corporate professional. Nevertheless, I was obedient. I felt as if that is what the Lord was telling me to do, and I wanted to honor Him. This is also one of the ways I grew in my ability to hear from God for myself. If you never act on what you believe God is saying, how will you ever know if it is really Him? We have to always practice hearing the voice of God.

Getting back to my story, for a while it seemed like nothing was happening. That is until one day I was at church serving and one of the administrators complimented me on the way I was dressed. I thanked her, and then proceeded to engage her in conversation. In doing so, I casually mentioned the reason I was dressed that way, pointing out the fact that I was dressing for the kind of job I wanted at the leading of the Holy Spirit. Fast forward to about a month later, this same administrator remembered our encounter and that I needed a job when someone reached out to her regarding an open job opportunity. Apparently, the woman was looking for referrals, and I came highly recommended. By God's design, after being unemployed for almost 6 months with no steady income, I finally had a job because of one small act of obedience that I could have written off as minor. Had I not been wearing those clothes, the administrator would have never known I was unemployed which means she would have never referred me.

This story does not end there. Let me explain. In this new role, I still was not wearing business clothes like I aspired to wear in my ideal role. However, that job gave me the experience that I needed for the next job that I would get just seven months later. When I started the new job, my salary tripled! Not doubled. tripled. And guess what? The company where I was hired has a very casual dress code for everyone except the department in which I was hired. In the department where I was hired, we had to wear, you guessed it, business attire. But if I had never done A, I would have never gotten to B, which eventually led me to C.

God is so funny. We never know how He is going to do it but trust me He has a plan. If we are willing to heed His voice, that plan will all come together for our good even when it does not look like it will, and even when we do not understand. God is waiting for you to listen and obey Him in every area so that He can bless you with what He's been trying to get to you all along.

Obedience in Your Dating Relationships

Your obedience to God should not have boundaries. You should not surrender to Him in one area but do things your way in another. One of the most neglected areas of obedience I have witnessed in the Body of Christ is the area of dating and relationships. Many people will ask God to bless them with a spouse, but some of those same people are not willing to surrender that area to Him. They are not willing to stop dating for a season or drop a guy they sense the Lord is telling them to let go of. They won't inquire of the Lord before accepting a date from a person. They will get all the way to the altar and attach God's name to the union without ever asking if the person was God's choice for their life. This should not be. If there is any area you want God's input in, it would be this area of who will become your spouse. This is the person you are supposed to spend the rest of your life with, and that decision will no doubt affect almost every other decision and circumstance in your life.

There was not one relationship post dedicating my life to Christ where God was silent. I don't mean that He audibly spoke, but He definitely had an opinion about every single guy I decided to involve myself with. Each time, He communicated with me in different ways, but each time He was trying to send the same message: That is not your husband. I will admit that I did not listen to his leadings and had to learn my lessons the hard way. Therefore, I would like to share 3 candid stories of how God was leading me with the hope it saves you time and heartbreak or maybe even confirm that you are headed in the right direction.

Through His Still Small Voice

The very first time I recall God speaking to me about a guy was very shortly after I re-dedicated my life to Him. I was so very immature in the things of God, and I was still learning to hear His voice. However, one night during a church service, I heard Him pretty clear. This new guy I was dating decided to join me in service, and everything was going pretty well at first. But towards the end of the night, I heard a still small voice whisper very matter-of-factly to me these words: "He's going to tell you that you're his wife." I wouldn't say this was an audible voice. It was more like when you hear your thoughts inside of your head, but a little different because it rises from a place deep within you so you know it's not your own. You tend to hear your regular thoughts inside your mind on a very surface level, but you will know when it is the still small voice of God because you will hear it originate from deep down within your heart or your "gut" (this is your spirit) and you will know it was not your idea at all.

As I tried to process what I had just heard, I was pretty shocked because, at that point, I had only known this guy for a week or two. At the same time, I was pretty excited because to me that meant that I had found my husband. Spoiler alert. He was not my husband. That is NOT what it meant at all. I will explain in a bit. Sure enough, when church was over, the guy walked me to my car and said he had something to tell me. At this point I'm thinking OMG this is it, he is really about to say it. He then proceeds to tell me that God spoke to him and told him that I am his wife. I should have run for the hills right then and there, but I didn't. I stuck around for a while. I dated this guy, almost compromised my purity for this guy, and was engaged to this guy for all of one day before ending it altogether.

Let me tell you where I went wrong. Even though I heard God tell me through that still small voice that "he was going to tell me I'm his wife", God never confirmed that I was indeed his wife, He just said that the guy was going to tell me that. God is very precise about the words He uses, and He wastes nothing. This was more of a warning from God letting me know what was about to occur, sort of like a heads up rather than a "this is what it is". Here's what I learned from that situation. If someone tells you that "God said" you are their wife (or if they tell you anything that God supposedly said for that matter), it should not be new news to you. Instead, it should be a confirmation meaning God should have already placed that on your heart or told you explicitly. That was the case for me when John told me that I was his wife. If you recall, God had already told me in preparation for when John approached me about it. I was prepared for what he was going to say. I had complete and total peace, and it was more like an "oh yeah I already know" rather than a "What? This is news to me."

Do not just take my word for it though. Let me give you an example from the Bible. In Acts Chapter 10 when God was about to make known the Good News of the gospel to the Gentiles, He gave a man named Cornelius a vision, and an angel advised him to send two men to call for Peter. Around this same time, in a completely different town, he was also giving Peter a vision and then explicitly told Peter that He was sending the men for him. In other words,

God was informing and preparing each party for the news that He was trying to convey so that it would be confirmation for both of them. Remember, up until that time, the Gospel was only for the Jewish people. Since this was such a new concept and a big thing to be announced, God knew that He had to have it confirmed in each individual so that there would be no doubting that this is in fact from the Lord.

So was that guy I was dating lying on God? I'm not sure. I tend to believe that he just missed it like we sometimes do. I just know that I will never rely on someone else's information from God. Instead, I will forever cultivate my relationship with Him because if I am in constant fellowship with Him, there is no reason why God wouldn't give me a heads up on these things beforehand.

Through Dreams

The second time I remember God trying to lead me in a relationship is with a guy who I thought might be the one. We discussed marriage regularly. He seemed to be in a real relationship with God. He knew his purpose, and it even seemed to line up with mine. Why wouldn't this be it, right? Wrong! After dating this guy for a little while, I had a dream. When God is trying to convey a message to me through dreams it is usually symbolic rather than literal, and it is usually after He has tried to speak to me in other ways to no avail. That was the case in this relationship. God had already been tugging at my heart to let this relationship go, but I did not listen because I didn't think I could ever find a better fit for me. That was a bad move on my part.

In the dream, I was escorted to the top of a high-rise office building where I met with some men in suits at a round table, sort of like a conference room. The men had on shades and everything. It felt like Men in Black, to be honest. It was sort of a comical scene, but I could tell the dream was very serious and the men meant business. As I sat down, the men stared intently at me with their hands folded on the desk and then began speaking to me. They said something to the effect of: "You have the potential to make a huge impact on the world, but if you continue with this guy you will mess it all up."

When I awoke from the dream, I immediately understood that it was from God along with the message He was trying to convey. I knew that this guy was not the one He had in mind for me, and God wanted me to end it. Unfortunately, I still did not listen. I know. Don't judge me. This guy and I continued dating for a little while longer until one day he broke up with me. He claimed the Lord told him to let me go, but that did not stop me from being hurt and heartbroken. I could've avoided all of that had I just listened to God's 1st, 2nd and 3rd warning, but I didn't. Thank God for His grace and His mercy though because He never gave up on me. In the same way, He will never give up on you.

Through Inner Peace

This is one of the most common ways in which God leads us. If we would learn to practice and adhere to the peace of God, then we would save ourselves a whole lot of trouble. What do I mean by inner peace? Have you ever been in a situation or in the middle of making a decision, but you didn't quite feel settled? Maybe you just didn't have a good feeling in your "gut" about it or "something" was telling you not to do it. That means that your peace was disturbed. That was the Holy Spirit attempting to lead you in the middle of the circumstance or decision. If you are born again, then you automatically have the Holy Spirit dwelling inside of you, and He is a Helper. The more we take heed to His leading and guiding, the more He will help, and the easier it will become to recognize Him. All of the previously mentioned ways God leads should always be accompanied with the peace of God, but the peace of God can stand alone. This is because other forms of leadings can be duplicated by Satan such as dreams or even voices. However, Satan has no control over the spirit of a born-again believer, and the peace of God is the Spirit of God bearing witness with your spirit. Proverbs 20:27 says, "The spirit of man is the candle of the Lord searching all the inward parts of the belly." A candle lights and leads the way when things are dark. They were especially used during the time the Bible was written. In the same way, God will communicate with your spirit and use it to help lead the way in your life and shed light on dark areas.

I recall reading an old journal where I was writing about a guy I was talking to at the time. He seemed to have some good things going for himself, he texted or contacted me every day and he seemed to be a real Believer. However, in the journal I was questioning if I should continue talking to him because something did not seem right. He hadn't done anything in particular to make me suspicious. I just did not have any PEACE to pursue a relationship with this person.

Sure enough, this situationship did not end well. It turns out, the guy was in a whole relationship, and I only found out because we happened to be at the same concert in a city where I didn't even live. We even parked in the same section and happened to be leaving out of the parking lot at the same exact time. I believe God orchestrated that account. I believe He wanted me to see that we had no future together. Once again, I should have broken it off when God was leading me earlier through the inward witness. Because I hadn't, the result once again was disappointment. This one didn't hurt as bad as the last one though because we were not even in a real relationship, but it's still no fun being lied to by someone you invested time in and saw as a prospective mate.

I am completely convinced that God will lead and guide us in our relationships if we allow Him to. In fact, He will lead us in every single area of our lives if we invite Him to do just that. Proverbs 3:6 reminds us to acknowledge Him in all of our ways and He will direct our paths. The thing about being led by God is you have to practice hearing from Him. The more time you spend with Him, and the more you cultivate a relationship with Him, the more proficient you will become in this.

You can probably pick your best friend's voice out of a sea of other voices. Why is that? It is because you have spent plenty of time with your best friend and you know them on an intimate level. God's voice will not be familiar to you if you have not learned how to filter it from all of the other voices in the world including your own voice as well as the voice of the enemy. Trust me, these days you NEED to know how to be led by God. It is not enough to read a section in a book titled "How You Will Know He's the One", as an example. It is great for reference, hence why I included it in the previous section, but you want to have the specifics for your situation, and God wants to help you with that. So lean into His voice, lean into His leading, and lean into total surrender to His will.

PART III

BECOMING

C H A P T E R 5

Growing in your relationship with God

As scary and intimidating as it may sound, cultivating a better, more intimate relationship with God does not have to be overwhelming. It is often those small, consistent steps in the right direction that will lead you to your end goal. What I know to be true is that a real, authentic, and personal relationship with Jesus is the foundation of everything that you have read and will read in this book. In other words, in order to walk into the full manifestation and to receive the God kind of results that I often speak about, you have to have the God that I often speak about first. You cannot know how to be led in your relationship if you do not know the One who leads. You cannot be found by the one if you do not know the One who first finds you and brings the two of you together. You will never know your true worth if you do not find it in the One who gives it to you. All roads lead back to Jesus, always.

When you build your life upon the solid rock of Jesus Christ, you can withstand whatever life throws your way. I love the picture that Jesus painted for us in the book of Matthew. "Therefore whoever hears these sayings of Mine, and does them, I will liken him to a wise man who built his house on the rock: and the rain descended, the floods came, and the winds blew and beat on that house; and it did not fall, for it was founded on the rock. "But everyone who hears these sayings of Mine, and does not do them, will be like a foolish man who built his house on the sand: and the rain descended, the floods came, and the winds blew and beat on that house, and it fell. And great was its fall." (Matthew 7:24-27)

I don't know about you, but I want my house to stand. I want my marriage to stand. I want my friendships to stand. I want my children to stand. I want my ministry to stand. I want my business to stand. I want my life to stand. For me to guarantee this, I will have to continue to cultivate my relationship with God and build upon the solid rock of His truths.

That being said, one thing that I can appreciate is that we are all at different places in our lives spiritually. You may have been in the faith for several years or just a few months. Maybe you were a believer at one point in time, but you sort of fell off and are trying to rebuild your relationship with God. Maybe you have not even begun your journey or you only know of God but don't quite know God for yourself. Wherever you fall on the spectrum, it is okay. The beautiful thing is that we are all running our own unique individual race, and the best thing we can do is stay in our own unique, individual lane while fixing our eyes on Jesus. He is the author and the finisher of our faith (Hebrews 12:2). No matter where you are in your walk with God, I think it is safe to say that none of us have arrived and that we could all benefit from more intimacy with Him.

For this reason, I would like to share some things that you can do to grow closer in your relationship with God. God promises that as we draw near to Him, He will draw near to us (James 4:8). So as you begin to take more steps in the right direction toward Him, I am positive you will begin to see Him show up more and more in every area of your life. You can use the following tools to refresh a relationship with Him that may have grown stale or jumpstart a relationship that you wish to begin. As you put them to use, keep in mind that you are building your life on the solid rock foundation that is Jesus Christ, and you will be well on your way to becoming a good thing before the ring.

Fast

Fasting is when you abstain from food and/or drink for spiritual purposes. Eventually, what happens is the time you would normally use to eat and drink, now becomes a time for prayer and/or the reading of the Word. You free up more time for devotion and giving your attention to the things of God. You are also denying your fleshly body (carnality) which in turn gives your spirit more of an opportunity to dominate. Fasting is one of the most powerful and often one of the fastest ways to cause things to happen here on earth. When the disciples asked Jesus why they could not cast the unclean spirit out of a young boy in Mark chapter 9 verse 29 , Jesus replied, "This kind can come out by nothing but prayer and fasting."

Jesus, Himself knew all about fasting. After all, when He was led into the wilderness to be tempted by the devil, He fasted for 40 days and 40 nights going without food. He came out full of power ready to begin His earthly ministry (Matthew 4). It is always interesting to me that Jesus did not even attempt to begin His ministry before having fasted. I tend to believe He knew there were some things He needed to get out of that season of denying His flesh and being consecrated unto His Father. I wonder how many new seasons we try to enter without first taking some time to fast and pray for God to pour into us and rid ourselves of all ungodly build-up? We are quick to say we want a "new season" and proclaim "God is doing a new thing," but we must also realize that God will not place new wine into old wineskins. "And no one putteth new wine into old bottles: else the new wine doth burst the bottles, and the wine is spilled, and the bottles will be marred: but new wine must be put into new bottles." (Mark 2:22).

People often believe that fasting moves the hand of God when in actuality, fasting moves us. And it is through the changing and realigning of some things in us that God can move and make things happen in our lives and the world around us.

I remember the very first time I fasted. I had no idea what I was doing. All I knew was that I needed a miracle, and I was willing to try anything. I did what some call a Daniel Fast based on Daniel 10:3. I was only allowed to consume fruits, vegetables, and other things that grew naturally in the earth. This may not seem like much nowadays especially with the growth of the vegan movement, but back then it was a huge deal, especially for someone like me whose diet consisted mainly of meat and dairy. I had never done anything like it, and apparently, God recognized my sacrifice because He came through in a major way.

My fast lasted the entire span of the lent season, which was over 40 days, but God granted me what I was praying for well before it was over although I continued to fast for the duration of the time. Shock and awe are not even enough to describe the state I was in. I laughed, I cried, I thanked God, praised Him, and cried some more. He did exceeding abundantly above all that I could ask or think. What is even better than Him answering my prayer though is that ever since that fast, my life was never the same. See, at the time I did the fast, I was not living completely for God. I had known Him as Savior, but not Lord over my life. I was still doing all types of worldly things including having premarital sex, clubbing, drinking excessively and more. I did, however, abstain from all of these things during the fast, which added to the sacrifice.

After the fast, even though I went back to those things for some time, something was different. I was convicted more easily, and it became harder for me to indulge in the sins and activities that I knew God was not pleased with. My conscience was more sensitive. Eventually, God abruptly moved me away from my hometown, and 6 months later I gave my life to the Lord for real. He radically saved me and in an instant, all of those sins that had me bound were completely gone. I was free. I was even able to abstain from sex until God sent me the man of my dreams. We only knew each other intimately in that way once we got married. One simple yet powerful act, the act of fasting, was the thing that I very strongly believe spawned every other one of these events. Fasting opened up the door for more. Fasting increased my capacity for Jesus. Fasting challenged the sin that was on the inside of me. Fasting increased my sensitivity to spiritual things. Fasting was the key.

There are many different types of fasts. This isn't a book about fasting so I will not get into all of those details, but I would highly suggest you research and figure out what is the best fast for you. The type, length, and all the other details are not that important (unless God gives you specific instructions concerning these areas). What is important is that your heart is in the right place. If it's a sacrifice for you, then it will be a sacrifice to God. He sees your heart, and He knows your intentions.

Journal

I may be a bit biased since I am an author and all, but I love expressing my thoughts through writing. I am usually much better at articulating with a pen and paper (or keyboard) than I am at speaking out loud. Whether or not you're the same way, journaling is a great way to express yourself to God. Journaling by hand gives you more time to think and express your thoughts as opposed to communicating audibly.

I usually start my journal entries with "Dear Daddy" (since God is my Father). It makes it more intimate and personal to me, but you can begin however you'd like. From there, I just write whatever comes to mind. Sometimes I write about things, people or situations that I am currently struggling with. Then there are other times when I just want to thank Him and express my gratitude. Sometimes it's questions I may have for Him. At times it's a revelation I received from reading the Word. Sometimes it turns into prayer. Whatever you decide to write is completely up to you. Do not overthink it. There are no rules. This is just another form of communication between you and God. It is also helpful for the times when you can't necessarily get any privacy to go away and talk to God on your own such as when you're on vacation with family. You will find journaling to be very freeing, and it can also bring you more clarity on situations. On several occasions, God has spoken to me right in the middle of writing a sentence. He honors any time that we devote to Him and journaling is a creative way to do just that.

Go to Church Regularly and Get Planted There

I know this is a no-brainer for some, but like I said we are all in different places on our walk with God so for others, the idea of going to church may not be so obvious. There is a reason that Hebrews 10:25 reminds us to not to forsake assembling together as believers. Here is that verse in the NIV: "not giving up meeting together, as some are in the habit of doing, but encouraging one another--and all the more as you see the Day approaching." There is something special that happens whenever believers gather together. We can encourage one another and help each other run our race. Sometimes we get weak and need an extra push, a friendly reminder, or a testimony from a sister or brother to help get us through. I can't tell you how many times my breakthroughs have come from something a sister in Christ has done or said or how many times a question I may have had for God was answered through the man of God in the pulpit. You cannot fully grow if you are not planted in a good church. A plant with no root eventually dies. Likewise, a believer who is not planted has no root and will eventually die spiritually.

I understand that people have many reasons for why they may not be attending church, but none of them are worth your progression in God. I know that church hurt is real. Shaming in some churches is real. Spiritual abuse is real. I understand that some preachers are not who they claim to be at all. However, Jesus is real and we have a responsibility to gather together to worship, hear His Word, and fellowship together as believers. If the church you used to attend isn't working out for you then do your due diligence to find one that will suit your needs. All churches are not the same. All preachers are not the same. All church people are not the same. Pray and ask God to lead you to the proper church where He sees fit for you to be planted.

He will direct your paths and lead the way if you allow Him, so no more excuses.

Romans 10:17 says "Faith comes by hearing, and hearing by the Word of God". Faith is a leaky substance. This means that even if you have heard the Word of God before and even if you got full of faith off of it, you still need to constantly put yourself in a position to hear in order to continue fueling your faith. If you are running low on faith then chances are you need to expose yourself to His Word on the particular subject that you are believing God for. So even when you cannot necessarily physically get to church, it is important to stay full of His Word through the many resources available to us today such as podcasts, YouTube, the Bible apps, streaming services and more.

Go on a Weekly Date with Jesus

Okay don't think I'm weird or anything, but I used to go on dates with Jesus all of the time when I was single. I do not have as much free time to do so now, but I still try to squeeze them in from time to time. I would get dressed up as if I was going on a regular date and spend some quality time with my Lord and Savior. A few date ideas would be going for a walk or picnic at the park, going out to lunch or dinner at a restaurant, or even having a movie night at home. Of course, you want to make sure that the movie of choice does not grieve the Holy Spirit and that you are guarding your heart.

Going on dates with Jesus is a good idea for anyone who may struggle with having an intimate friendship with God. It takes you out of the traditional, systematic way of doing things and gets you into the habit of talking to God as if He is right there with you because the truth is, He is right there with you. If you plan to have your date in a public place and you don't want people to think you are crazy, you can also bring a journal to write down your thoughts and things you hear from God. Just like married people should go on regular date nights or date days, the believer needs to be intentional about their relationship with Christ by connecting with Him regularly as we are His bride according to Ephesians 5.

Listen to Praise and Worship Music

Sometimes drawing closer to Jesus isn't even that deep. Sometimes we just need to purge ourselves of some of the things we are watching and listening to and replace it with something more edifying. It helps us to think better, to gain more clarity, and to hear from God more. Put in some headphones or grab a Bluetooth speaker and blast your favorite gospel, praise, or worship music. There is just something about the headphones or speaker because you hear the music clearer and it seems to touch you more. If you are not in the middle of your room on your face, tears forming and snot falling then you are not doing it right. Stay right there until you can feel the manifested presence of God. Believe me, He will show up. He inhabits the praises of His people (Psalm 22:3) and we were created to worship Him. My sweetest worship sessions were not during the praise and worship set at a church service or a ministry's conference. Instead, some of my greatest moments and most powerful breakthroughs were birthed in the privacy of my home right in the middle of my bedroom, living room, and kitchen.

Get an Accountability Partner

If you want to take your journey with God seriously then you need an accountability partner. This is a person who you trust that will hold you accountable in your walk with God. You have to be able to trust this person because if they need to tell you about yourself then you are going to have to know that their motives are pure, their heart is in the right place and their love for you is genuine. If you do not know this for sure then it may be hard for you to receive from them and the relationship will not be effective. Find someone who you are not going to have a hard time being honest with and someone who you will not feel judged by, but who does not mind lovingly correcting you if needed.

Typically, accountability partners are on the same or similar levels spiritually so that they can hold one another accountable and journey together, but this is not always the case. An accountability partner can also be a mentor, spiritual mother, pastor, etc. Some of the things you may use your accountability partner for include checking in on you if you are struggling with an addiction in a certain area, being a sounding board if you find yourself in any difficult circumstances as well as checking in on you if you are going out on a date to make sure you're back home at a decent time and not doing anything crazy. An accountability partner may also check in on you if you stop attending church for any reason as well as a host of other things. We all need someone in our lives to be this kind of person for us no matter what season we find ourselves in because no one person is an island, and we are all better when we are doing life together. It would be very challenging if you were trying to draw closer to God without friends or people who were on the same path as you. It's not impossible, but having it certainly makes the journey easier, more enjoyable and more likely to succeed.

Read Your Bible Every Single Day

This may be another no-brainer, but again we are all in different places spiritually and even the most mature believer can struggle to read their Bible every day. Psalm 119:105 says "Your Word is a lamp unto my feet, and a light unto my path". That means the more you read God's Word, the more things in your life will become illuminated. The light of His Word has the power to do miraculous things in our lives, especially draw us closer to our Creator. Jesus Himself is the Word (John 1). It is imperative that we spend as much time with the Word as possible.

There are many resources that we have access to nowadays right at our fingertips. I am especially fond of the YouVersion Bible app which includes free devotionals and Bible plans on almost any subject. As American Christians, we have the privilege of being able to practice our faith openly which also includes being able to carry and read our Bibles. I can admit, sometimes I take this for granted, but it should not be this way. There is now no excuse not to read your Bible every day. You just need to purpose in your heart that you are going to do it, and then take the time to do so. If you make the Word of God a priority you will begin to see great growth in your life both spiritual and otherwise.

Write scriptures on sticky notes and post them around your house

Doing this exercise does not count as reading your Bible every day because you want focused, quality time reading, studying, or meditating on the Word. However, this is a very helpful tool to improve the quality of your spiritual life. If we have scriptures posted and constantly within our view, we are more likely to think about God or react differently when situations and circumstances arise. Whatever is going in, must come out, and if we are full of the word, that fullness will overflow when we need it most.

That is why I suggest posting sticky notes in places you frequent such as mirrors, the bathroom, the refrigerator, etc. I had sticky notes virtually everywhere in my apartment when I was going through a tough season financially. I needed to trust God wholeheartedly. As a result, I posted scriptures that spoke to my spirit and my situation and it helped to keep me grounded. I would often recite them out loud when I passed by one or if I was having a tough day. It is a great exercise to try no matter where you are in your relationship with God.

Get rid of something in your life that you know is hindering you or separating you from God

You cannot grow close to someone if there is a wedge between the two of you. No matter what efforts are made to draw closer by either party, if there is something there, it will no doubt get in the way of full intimacy. For some of us, this may be an egregious sin and for others, it may be as simple as a bad habit. For others, you may need to get rid of a person or a relationship that is not edifying. Whatever that thing is that you're thinking about right now, that's it. Just do it. Don't even think about it. Just get rid of it, and watch your relationship with God, and your life, in general, take a turn for the better.

Pray more

As simple as "pray more" seems, many of us fail to make it a priority. Oftentimes, we make excuses for not praying enough citing things such as not having enough time or not knowing exactly what to pray, but the truth is we cannot afford to skip out on prayer-ever. First Thessalonians 5:17 says to pray without ceasing, which means we should be praying all the time about everything.

Prayer is communication with God. It is an opportunity for us to partner with Him for His will to be done here on earth. If we are not praying, then how will His will for our lives and the lives of others ever take place? It is not going to happen because you posted an Instagram post saying it will. It will not happen because you wrote it down on a piece of paper. It will happen because you prayed and asked God and you believed Him in faith. The more you communicate with God, the more you will know Him. The more you know Him, the more you will want to know Him. The more you hunger and thirst after Him, the more you will be filled.

When you pray often, you will also come to the place where you can clearly discern the voice of God. You will know Him and you will know His voice because you have been in communication with Him regularly. That is what we call *relationship*. God longs for a relationship with you. A deep, loving, meaningful relationship that cannot be shaken or tossed to and fro by the ebbs and flows of life. One that is built on the solid foundation of the rock of His love. It is in the place of prayer that you will find rest for your soul, direction for your life, answers to your questions and the priceless gift of God's presence.

Pray in the Spirit

This one is a game-changer. I know beyond a shadow of a doubt that praying in the Spirit has supercharged my spiritual life and changed my natural life for the better. This may be the missing link you have been looking for and the key to a richer, fuller relationship with God. What I mean by praying in the Spirit in this context is speaking in tongues. This is available to every believer. You do not have to be someone in the fivefold ministry or have a special gift to speak in tongues for your personal edification. Keep in mind that there is also a gift of speaking in tongues which is for the edification of the church. This type of tongues requires interpreting (either by the one who gave the tongue or by another). Every believer does not have this gift. Here are a few scriptures that reference praying in the Spirit:

> Praying always with all prayer and supplication in the Spirit, and watching thereunto with all perseverance and supplication for all saints -Ephesians 6:18

> But ye, beloved, building up yourselves on your most holy faith, praying in the Holy Ghost -Jude 20

> What is it then? I will pray with the spirit, and I will pray with the understanding also: I will sing with the spirit, and I will sing with the understanding also.- 1 Corinthians 14:15 For if I pray in an [unknown] tongue, my spirit prayeth, but my understanding is unfruitful. -1 Corinthians 14:14

All of these scriptures reference speaking in tongues in the context of praying in the Spirit.

From the scriptures, we can pull out some of the key features and benefits of speaking in tongues. In the book of Jude, we learn that praying in the Spirit builds us up on the inside. "But you, beloved, building yourselves up on your most holy faith, praying in the Holy Spirit." -Jude 1:20 I like to think of it as recharging my spiritual battery. Whenever I am feeling spiritually dull or worn out, I spend some time praying in the Spirit and I never fail to feel recharged after doing so.

In 1 Corinthians 14, we learn from Paul that when we pray in the Spirit, we are not speaking to man, but God, and many times we will have no idea what we are even saying in the Spirit so it is a good idea to pray both in the spirit and in our natural tongue. We pray in the Spirit because obviously, it has some supernatural benefits that praying in our understanding does not. We pray in our understanding because at least we know what we are saying which makes our understanding more fruitful. There are benefits to both. For he who speaks in a tongue does not speak to men but to God, for no one understands *him;* however, in the spirit, he speaks mysteries. For if I pray in a tongue, my spirit prays, but my understanding is unfruitful. What is *the conclusion* then? I will pray with the spirit, and I will also pray with the understanding. I will sing with the spirit, and I will also sing with the understanding. 1 Corinthians 14:2; 14-15

Finally, from Romans 8:26-27, we gather that when we don't quite have the words to say or when we don't know what to pray, we can pray in the Spirit and the Spirit will pray out God's will. "And the Holy Spirit helps us in our weakness. For example, we don't know what God wants us to pray for. But the Holy Spirit prays for us with groanings that cannot be expressed in words. And the Father who knows all hearts knows what the Spirit is saying, for the Spirit pleads for us believers, in harmony with God's own will." (NLT)

I understand that for some people, speaking in tongues may be strange. However, there is nothing strange or spooky about the Holy Spirit. When I was a new believer, I had the same misconception, but when I asked Him to fill me up as I was in the middle of a new membership class at my church, He did. Since then, my life has never been the same. So, if you want to receive, take some time to ask God to fill you, He is not trying to withhold the fullness of the Holy Spirit from you.

"So I say to you, ask, and it will be given to you; seek, and you will find; knock, and it will be opened to you. For everyone who asks receives, and he who seeks finds, and to him who knocks it will be opened. If a son asks for bread from any father among you, will he give him a stone? Or if *he asks* for a fish, will he give him a serpent instead of a fish? Or if he asks for an egg, will he offer him a scorpion? If you then, being evil, know how to give good gifts to your children, how much more will *your* heavenly Father give the Holy Spirit to those who ask Him!" (Luke 11:9-13)

Pure Heart. Clean Hands

You mustn't just seek God's hands. We should always first and foremost be after His heart. God sees our hearts. (1 Samuel 16:7) So, if our motives for coming to Him is to gain a husband or anything else besides wanting a true relationship with Him, then we will not get very far. It is perfectly okay for the goodness of God to be our expectation because we know that He is a rewarder of them that diligently seek Him (Hebrews 11:6), but it should never be our reason. The great thing is, we can always pray and ask God to show us our hearts and our motives and then pray for Him to help us to change. Philippians 2:13 says, "For God is working in you, giving you the desire and the power to do what pleases Him. (NLT) I use this scripture every time I pray about something I want to change in me because it lets us know that not only does God give us the desire to do what is right, but He also gives us the power to do it. All we have to do is receive and walk in that truth.

My prayer is that you would come to know the love of Christ that surpasses knowledge, that you may be filled with all the fullness of God. (Ephesians 3:19)

CHAPTER 6

Single & Whole

I often hear couples bragging about how they married their "other" half, and it always makes me cringe a little on the inside to hear those words. To me, to marry your other half implies that you were not already whole before you got married. The best kind of couple is one consisting of two whole individuals coming together to become one flesh. The way God sees it, one plus one equals one. Instead of looking for someone to complete you, you should be patiently waiting for the one who will complement you. Don't misunderstand me. Your spouse should inspire you to be a better person, challenge you, and improve your overall quality of life. However, your completion is an assignment reserved only for God.

There is a difference between being complete and being perfect. Perfection is a mark that we press towards (Philippians 3:12), but one that cannot be achieved until Christ returns (Philippians 1:6). What I do not want is for you to assume that you have to have your whole life together and be a perfect individual before you get married. The truth is, you will not be perfect before you get married, and you certainly will not be perfect after. We are being perfected every single day of our walk. Instead, you should seek to be mentally, emotionally, and spiritually healthy. That is the recipe for wholeness.

It is important that you are truly enjoying your season of singleness. The thing about seasons is that they are temporary. We know without a doubt there will always be a winter, spring, summer, and autumn as long as the earth remains. Seasons change. So it is with our life. You may be single right now, but one day you will wake up and your husband will be lying next to you. I do not want you to waste this season. I do not want you to be so zealous about getting to your next that you fail to take in the beauty of the now. Us humans are something else. For some reason, we find it hard to truly sit in the beauty of each season without rushing it out of our year. For example, we complain all winter about how cold it is then when summer comes around and brings the heat, we wish we would have appreciated how much cooler it was. The truth is every season comes with its share of beauty as well as its share of challenges. Therefore, it is up to us to appreciate and be content with our portion, whatever it may be at the time.

One of the reasons why it is so important to be whole in God before getting married is because marriage is going to bring with it its own set of adjustments. If you are not strong, complete, and secure in God and who He has called you to be, you could potentially have a more challenging time adjusting. Some people even find themselves going through a mini-identity crisis. Okay, that sounds a bit dramatic. This isn't like the mid-life crisis that drives 40 something-year-old men to purchase a new red Corvette. It's not even a quarter-life crisis that many young people seem to be experiencing nowadays. A more appropriate term would probably be an "identity transition". What do

I mean by identity transition? Well, if you have made the transition from being stuck in the bondage of sin to giving your life over to Christ and living fully for Him then chances are you have been through a period where you have endured transition and maybe even a bit of uncertainty in the area of your identity. When you live for the world, the world has a certain way of operating, but when you live for God and His kingdom, then there is a completely opposite way of living and operating. But underneath all of that, there is still YOU.

Still don't get it? Well, let me just speak for myself then. Before Christ, I was trap music-loving, club-hopping, drinking, cursing Rita but those things shouldn't be carried over into a godly life, right? But what about other things like the unique things that made me-*me* such as the fact that I love to dress up and look nice, or the fact that I love dancing. What about the fact that I'm an introvert and all of the other unique things that made me- *me*? Do I still dress like that? Can I still think like this? Can I still talk like that? I didn't exactly know how to grapple with all of those things and navigate through it all. There were so many tendencies and character flaws that I was losing and getting rid of to where I felt stripped down to my essence and I had to really see myself (in Christ) and then slowly add back layers. Well, that's sort of what happens when you get married but on a bit of a smaller scale.

My BFF said something profound to me one day. She told me that she was finally figuring out who Maygen Blake is- that's her maiden name. She then went on to explain that she now has to figure out who Maygen King is- that's her married name. I didn't quite grasp the full magnitude of what she was trying to convey back then, but now that I have been married for five years at the time of this writing, I finally get it. I am still trying to figure out who Rita Brooks is. I am not confused or anything by any means, but I feel as though I am still transitioning into her, and I am okay with that because this is a journey, and I have an entire lifetime to figure out and be Mrs. Brooks. The important thing is that I got through that first identity transition-the one where I had to allow God to show me who I am in Him. That is a part of the process of becoming whole. Who are you without all of your titles, your degrees, your positions, your status? If you can get a firm grasp on that, then you are in a good place of wholeness in Christ. If you are not quite sure, ask God to show you who you are in Him. He will help you so that nothing or no one else can ever define you again.

Purposed

Part of being whole in Christ and knowing your identity is allowing God to give you purpose. Nothing awakens a person more than being fully aware of why they were put here on the earth. Purpose is one of the first things God ignited in me when I dedicated my life back to Him. He placed such a strong desire in my heart to seek Him for my purpose, and I am still seeking and learning to humbly yet boldly and confidently walk in it every day. My desire to fulfill my purpose was even stronger than my desire to be found by a man, and I do not believe it was a coincidence that during the season when I was fervently praying about walking in my purpose, God brought my husband. Why do you think that is? It is because my husband is a huge part of my purpose, and God knew that my heart was genuine to walk in what He has called me to do.

When you find purpose, you find a greater reason for living and every day becomes a new opportunity to carry it out. You realize that life is bigger than just you, and there is a beautiful almost unexplainable feeling that comes with walking and living it out. God,

Himself, is so very purpose-driven. He does not do anything "just because" including bringing individuals together for marriage. While you may be thinking how much better life would be if you had a man to come home to at night, God is thinking on a whole other level. When He puts two people together in the precious covenant of marriage, He has a purpose for that union. Sure, the byproduct of that is the happiness and romance of two people in love, but His plans and His purpose are so much greater. If you do not even know your purpose, how are you supposed to vet a man of God who approaches you? Both of you must know your individual purposes so that you can determine if the relationship will even make sense.

The fact that your relationship may look good on paper means absolutely nothing. You must also ask yourself if your purpose aligns with his. Remember, this does not mean that your purposes must be the same. What it does mean, however, is that your purposes must complement each other's because a wife is called to be the helpmeet and aid in the vision of her husband. Ultimately, the way to truly know if your purposes align is to ask God. He knows both of you and He knows what He has planned for your lives.

If you are not quite sure what your purpose is, a great place to start is to make a list of the things you love to do, the things you are passionate about, and the things you are good at. Then allow God to speak to you. I also like to ask 2-3 of the closest people to me what they think I'm good at and find the similarities. I guarantee you that the key to your purpose is somewhere in the intersection of the things you write down on that list. Remember that purpose is different from assignment. All of us have an overarching purpose of bringing people to Jesus. Your individual purpose is in *how* you will uniquely accomplish that using the gifts God has given you. The assignments are the individual tasks along the way in each season that help you fulfill your unique purpose.

Emotionally Whole

One of the hardest things to go through in life is a breakup with someone you loved and once cared about. Somehow, I had managed to go through 25 years of life without experiencing that kind of heartbreak, but that didn't make the pain of it all any more bearable when it did come rearing its ugly head during the Fall of 2012. I never saw it coming either. When the guy told me he wanted to end things, I thought sure he was just being dramatic and would change his mind in a few days once he realized what (and who) he was losing. Well, that day never came, and I was left to face my demons...alone. That began one of the hardest seasons of my life. Not only did I get broken up with for the first time in life, but this was also the season when I felt the Lord leading me to leave law school without having any idea what I was supposed to do next. I need you to understand, I was manless, schoolless, jobless, purposeless and I felt worthless. I thought this whole walking with Jesus thing was supposed to make my life better, not worse, yet there I was in a semi-depressive state because of everything that was happening (or wasn't happening) around me.

Honestly, part of me tried to block that season out of my mind because it was just so hard, but another part tries to keep those memories alive to remember just how far the Lord has brought me. Either way, there was one day, in particular, I will never forget. On that particular day, I came across a Bible verse I had never seen before (I was still pretty new to this whole walking with God thing). This is what that verse says in the New Living Translation: *I am the true grapevine, and my Father is the gardener. He cuts off every branch of mine that doesn't produce fruit, and He prunes the branches that do bear fruit so they will produce even more. -John 15:1-2.* It was as if the words on the page of my little Life Application Bible were jumping right out at me. I sat up in my bed and said out loud as if there was someone else in the room with me "OMG, He's pruning me". The lightbulb had turned on, the revelation had come and I had been enlightened.

I then proceeded to look up what pruning meant. I found out that pruning is an essential part of the gardening process. It encourages healthy growth but requires all of the bad stuff to be cut off for the plant's true beauty to come forth. If God is pruning you, just know that you did not necessarily do anything wrong. On the contrary, it likely means that He is pleased with you and you have been doing something right. John 15:2 tells us that He only prunes the branches that are already bearing fruit. Why? So that they can produce even more fruit. You would think that with all of the revelation God had given me on that scripture that it would have made that season a little easier right? Well, it didn't. I didn't want to be cut, but I knew that for God to pull out my full potential and get the most glory from my life, I had to lean into the pruning, not pull back from it.

That lightbulb moment led me to make one of the maturest decisions in my walk with God. I decided I was no longer going to date, and I refrained from interacting with all guys for an entire year. The only time I did so was at group events for church and even then, I kept myself from one on one interactions as to not come off as flirtatious or romantically interested. I didn't want any man to get the wrong idea.

I needed some time to become whole. I wanted to take some time and work on myself in every aspect. I wanted to get my mind right, my emotions right, my spirit right, my temple right, my cash right (hello somebody?!) before I even thought about bringing another person into the mix. Many times, we are so focused on what a person can do for us, but I wanted to be sure that I was bringing the best possible version of myself to them. Secondly, I was very tired of the "dating" cycle I was in (and I use that word very loosely because I can only remember going on a handful of actual dates). After the guy completely rejected me for wanting to wait until marriage for sex, the 24-hour engagement that ended in a failed relationship, and my first real heartbreak, I was just ready to take a step back and do some reevaluation.

Something deep inside of me knew that it didn't have to be all of that, and if I could just recalibrate and hide in God, I could see things more clearly. I never thought that it would be a year. I didn't have a specific amount of time. I just told myself that I would know when it was time and when I was ready. All I knew is that doing it my way was getting me nowhere at all, and so I decided that this time I would try it God's way once and for all. There comes a certain point where you have to look at certain areas in your life that tend to go awry and say ok, maybe it's not them, or it, or that. Maybe it's me, and maybe I just need to take a step back for a second to get more insight.

How I Got Over the BreakUp

Erykah Badu was on to something when she told us to pack light. It's a good idea to leave as much baggage behind and let God heal you from some things that have taken root in your heart as a result of well.....life. Life can be straight-up hard sometimes, and if we are not careful to take the time to heal from certain things, we will just continue to live our lives putting a band-aid over the scars of our hearts, and carrying on like nothing ever happened. Eventually, you will just blow up and wonder where it all came from. Stop taking all that junk from relationship to relationship. Getting a man will not just make it all go away and you will not just live happily ever after.

You never want to go into a relationship expecting that person to be your god. People make terrible gods. They will disappoint you many times. You will find that once you get married, any and every issue that you never dealt with will begin to surface and you will be forced to deal with it. I like to think of it as a magnifying glass. In marriage, every single thing will be magnified to the nth degree, and then you will have no choice but to face your demons.

So how did I get over my breakup? Well, first I did not jump into another relationship right away. As I previously mentioned, the very next person I would end up being in a relationship with is my now-husband after my little one-year hiatus. DO NOT go the rebound route. Jumping into a relationship with another person right away will not make you feel better. You may think it will make you happy, but it won't. It will probably just make you feel empty all over again. Many times, we're immediately jumping into the next relationship because we just don't want to deal with the pain of it all, and sometimes we're just trying to make the previous guy jealous. Let me let you in on a secret. Promise not to get offended. OK...here goes...He IS NOT CHECKING FOR YOU BOO. He could probably care less about who you are dating now. If he realized what he had, he would have stayed in that relationship with you.

You will never be the right one to the wrong person. So stop accepting dates from random guys just so you can feel better about yourself. Stop posting pictures on social media hoping that he will creep on your page and see how great your life is going without him. Speaking of social media, stop going on his page. Unfollow him on all social media, and block him if you have to. Yes, it's that serious; your healing is at stake. Also, have your friends unfriend and unfollow him too because you don't need them coming back to you reporting everything they see, and we don't need you grabbing their phone to creep on his page either. You will never be free from that man if you continue to concern yourself with his life. So delete his number and move on. It will take time to heal completely, but you are adding more time on that clock every time you click on his username so just stop it. Take control of your life and just hit delete on any and everything that bears his name.

Secondly, it may be time to stop listening to love songs and watching sad and/or romantic movies. You may think I'm taking it too far. What is wrong with love songs? You may ask. I mean it's not trap music. What is wrong with romantic movies? At least it's not murder and violence. Well, 1 Corinthians 10:23 KJV says this: "All things are lawful for me, but all things are not expedient: all things are lawful for me, but all things edify not." Paul was trying to explain that although some things are not sinful, it does not mean that that thing is good for you. Everything is not advantageous to your growth and your life in general. That is why it is so important to be led by the Holy Spirit in your everyday walk with Christ. He will tell you things you should do and things you shouldn't. He will let you know if you should give something up or if you should do more of something. The more you listen and follow His leadings, the more He will lead and guide you. Likewise, the more you ignore Him, the more His voice will be suppressed and it will be harder for you to hear from Him.

So about these love songs and movies....You have to be ever so careful about what you are letting into your ear gates and your eye gates. Proverbs 4:23 NIV says "ABOVE ALL guard your heart with all diligence for out of it flows the issues of life." I don't know about you, but if the Bible is saying *above all* that means it is pretty important, and I need to pay attention. This verse is commonly misinterpreted. It does not tell us to close our hearts off to people. It is letting us know that we have to be diligent about what we are letting into our hearts or our spirits. It implies keeping a watch over it and being diligent about what we allow to enter. How do we let things in? Through our ear and eye gates meaning what we listen to and what we watch. It says for out of it flows the issue of life. This means things are coming out of us and manifesting in our lives and yet we are wondering where it is coming from. We fail to realize, it is coming from what we are letting get into our hearts through our ears and eyes. You have all types of anger issues, getting upset with someone out of nowhere, not realizing it's because of that show you just watched. Or you're all depressed and sad out of nowhere not realizing it's because of that song you had on repeat the other day. Then you have the nerve to blame it on the devil. No boo some things we unknowingly bring on ourselves. You may think it's not that serious, but it is. Every time we are listening and watching things especially repeatedly and over long periods of time, that is a form of meditation. We are meditating on those things and whatever goes in must come out.

Listen, when I got this revelation during my single season, I stopped listening to R&B and love songs. It would put me in all types of moods. Sometimes it would put me in a sad or depressed mood. Other times, it would bring me back to a particular relationship, because there is something about music that makes us nostalgic. We remember certain seasons and situations in our lives based on the songs that were prevalent then or the ones we listened to the most or at a particular moment in our life. These things are powerful. I still do not listen to many of the so-called love songs even now that I am married, and if I do I am very selective. If you just sit and listen to some of the lyrics in the songs you will understand why. I know that my words are powerful and some of the things these songs are saying I just do not want to confess over my life and my relationship. If God is tugging on your heart right now pointing out something in particular just listen to Him. He is only trying to set you up for success. Do not harden your heart.

Next, focus on bettering yourself and doing things you are passionate about. One of the reasons I took this particular break-up so hard is because other things in my life were going on at the time that was shaking up my entire word and life as I knew it. Specifically, I had just left law school after being led by the Lord to do so, leaving me feeling empty and worthless. I did not know who I was apart from this man and especially apart from my academic achievements. I had not yet discovered my identity or my purpose, and so every single ounce of worth and self-esteem I had was dependent upon superficial things. God had to strip me of everything in that pruning season so that I could become who I was in Him and not in anything or anyone else. He was then able to build me back up again with Christ as my solid foundation- a foundation that can never be shaken. Now my worth is not in a man, a career, my education, degrees, my titles, labels, relationship status, the clothes I wear, or any other fleeting thing. Once you find out what you are placed on this earth to do, once you figure out your passion and what God has gifted you with, pursue Him and pursue it, and you will be consumed with so much joy and purpose, and fulfillment that you will not have time to waste tears over a man who probably never knew your worth in the first place.

Lastly, allow yourself *time* to get over the heartbreak. Some wounds honestly just need time to heal, but if you keep opening the wound and adding salt to it with some of the things I mentioned earlier, you are just going to prolong the healing process which in turn, will prolong you being presented to the man God has selected just for you. Pray and worship your way through it. You will be surprised how small your problems become when you set an atmosphere of worship and truly encounter a BIG God.

Your journey to being whole is not one that will come overnight, but it doesn't have to take a long time either. God can redeem the time for you just as He did for me. So don't beat yourself up over your past mistakes, failures, and setbacks. Decide today that you are going to walk into your next relationship and ultimately your marriage as a whole person-whatever that means and whatever that looks like for you.

So, what happened after I came out of my little hiatus? Well, right around the 1-year mark I began to feel a release. I just knew that I was released to actually be open to the possibility of love and romance again and begin dating again-this time with the Lord's blessing. I knew I had learned so much about myself and more importantly about God, and it felt as though I was viewing the world through completely different lenses, giving me a brand new perspective. I still did not go out chasing a relationship though because I knew that it is he who finds a wife finds a good thing, not the other way around.

A few months after I began feeling like I was ready, an opportunity presented itself, and in typical life fashion, it was a counterfeit-a test to see if I really did learn the lessons. But just 3 months after that, the real thing presented itself. God removed the veil that was over me, opened my husband's eyes to me and the rest is history. John was in my church worshiping with me, serving with me, going to the same events as me and so much more for 2 WHOLE YEARS, but I was not ready. Neither of us were. But that year off put me in a position to be ready at just the right time. When it seemed like I was losing so much (potential mates, free dinners, shallow good times), the truth is I was gaining so much more.

C H A P T E R 7

Let's Talk About Sex

When I gave my heart to God in 2012 and decided that I was going to live for Him for real, that included saving myself for marriage. I made a vow to God that I would abstain from having sex and save my body for the man He had reserved for me. At the time, I didn't know anyone who had ever done this before, and I was not even sure if or how I was going to pull this off. As a matter of fact, the same day I rededicated myself, I had gone to church with a guy that I had just slept with the night before. The two of us were not even in a real relationship. All I knew was that abstaining from sex was a part of the package of submitting my life to God. He was calling me to a life of complete and total surrender to Him, and I no longer wanted to be in partial obedience.

The first thing I did was cut off the pseudo-relationship with the guy I was seeing at the time; the same one who came to church with me that day. He begged me to continue seeing him, even saying that he would be willing to do the whole abstinence thing with me. Most women would have taken him up on that offer, and I'll be honest, it was tempting. But in my heart, I knew that was the wrong move to make. First off, I was new to this whole God thing, so I did not want any distractions. Developing my walk with God was like a new relationship in and of itself. You know how it is when you begin dating someone you really really like. You spend every ounce of free time you have with that person, and all you want to do is get to know them better. If I would have continued talking to that guy, one of the relationships would have been neglected, either the one with God or the one with him. My new-found relationship with God was way too important for me to take that chance. I wanted to finally give God a fair shot; He deserved that much after all He had done for me.

Secondly, I had enough wisdom (even being fresh off the altar) to know that him trying out the whole abstinence thing was never going to work. It was not because he wasn't being genuine, and it's not even because I didn't think he could do it. It was because his motives were wrong. If a man decides that he is going to give up or do something just to please a woman, it will never last. That is so important I must repeat it again to make sure you understand. Anything a man does or tries to change for a woman and not for himself, even if it works temporarily WILL NOT LAST. That man has to be abstaining from sex because it is his personal conviction, and he is doing it to please the Lord. That is the only way it will last. The minute it gets hard or the woman does something to make him mad, sad or frustrated, what foundation does he have to stand on? His reasoning for making the change in the first place was not his idea, and so it cannot and will not be sustained. Even if a guy has the best intentions, which I am sure was the case in my situation, do not count on anyone to change because of you. This is why it is important that any guy you are courting already has his own convictions regarding abstaining until marriage. It is also best that he is already waiting out of honor and obedience to God. If it's something that he is not already doing (for a solid amount of time) and you all have to talk through it, then you may be setting yourself up for frustration down the road.

Speaking of motives, you have to know why you are choosing to abstain. Check your own motives as well. Are you doing it just because you heard that's what it takes to get a good man or some other shallow reason? Are you doing it because you think it will earn you a husband as a reward from God? Or are you doing it because you know that you were bought with a price and that you should glorify God in your body? (1 Corinthians 6:20). When things get tough and you want to give up, you are going to need a strong foundation to help sustain you, and if you always go back to your why, you will have greater success if your why is built on a solid foundation.

Why Wait

There is a reason God has reserved sex for the confines of a marriage union only. I think that sometimes we have this idea in our head that God is trying to control us and suck all of the fun out of our lives when in actuality, He puts certain boundaries in place for our good. He is the creator of all things, including us, which means He knows how we operate, and He knows the consequences of every action. When we engage in the act of sex, we are connecting with someone on a much deeper level than just physical. Sex is a very spiritual act, and as such, should only be shared between a man and his wife. We have been so desensitized and have turned an act that is supposed to be sacred into just another thing that we do for fun and pleasure.

Soul ties are real, and whenever you connect with someone physically, especially on numerous occasions over a prolonged period of time, you will find that your soul has become knitted to that person in a way that is unhealthy and damaging to your life. Since I have been on both sides of the fence (dating with sex and dating without sex), I can tell you that there is a tremendous difference between a break-up with someone you have had sex with and a person with whom you have not been intimate. I previously mentioned my first real relationship heartbreak came from a guy I began dating the summer after I got saved. We talked a lot about marriage and our plans for the future. The breakup left me lonely, broken, and empty. Like I stated before, I was already having a tough time in other areas in my life, so this break-up only added to the crushing blow that I thought would take me out. I'm no psychologist or anything and I was never clinically diagnosed, but I'm pretty sure I was on the brink of depression. There were days when I did not care to get out of bed. The entire world around me seemed so gray, and I could not seem to catch even a glimpse of sunshine. I could not see a light at the end of that dark tunnel, and so it was hard for me to believe people when they told me that things would get better.

As bad as it was though, it was not as bad as I know it could have been. As much as I had given to this person emotionally, I never gave my body to him physically. I was hurt, badly, but as bad as the heartbreak was, it did not take much time for me to get over this guy and move on with my life. And once I was over him, that was it. There was no going back or wondering what could have been. I just kept it moving with a clean slate and no ill feelings towards him at all. This was a stark contrast to my relationships pre-abstinence. Take my relationship with my high school sweetheart for example. This relationship dragged on way longer than it should have, and I withstood things in that relationship that no woman should ever have to endure. Even after the formal relationship was over, I would still find myself and my life intertwined with his in one way or another. I would even go on to have other relationships only to break it off and come back to him. It was a feeling I just could not shake. Something kept drawing me back to him even though the relationship was full of turmoil and clearly at a dead end. See, I had given him my body. Over and over again, my body and his connected on a level that was supposed to be reserved only for holy matrimony. It was not until I did that 40 day fast that changed my life that I was able to completely move past my past with him. I believe that somewhere during that fast, the soul tie was broken and I was completely free. Thank God!

When sex is a factor in a relationship, it tends to complicate things and causes our vision and judgment to be clouded. We can no longer judge soberly. Sex adds another layer to a relationship that was never supposed to be added in dating or courting relationships. Do yourself a favor and choose not to subject yourself to soul ties and all of its effects. The only soul you should want to be connected to in that way, and the only flesh you should desire to become one with is that of your husband once the two of you have been legally married in the sight of God.

Purity is about more than just the act of sex. I truly believe that God honors us when we honor Him, and He showed me just that when I decided to honor Him and keep even my actions pure before Him. When John and I were still courting, he made President's Club with his company and was awarded an all-inclusive trip to a Sandals resort in Jamaica. I was excited because he was given the option to bring a guest along for the trip, so who else would he take besides me, his new fiancée right?! Wrong! We were quickly convicted. I thought it would be cool as long as he slept on the couch and left me to sleep in the bed by myself. I was wrong. God made it clear that I was not to go on that trip.

I reluctantly but willingly gave up a free trip to Jamaica. Did I mention everything was paid for including the plane tickets? It hurt to give that trip up, I'm not going to lie. I even had a little brat moment where I cried, and not just necessarily because of this trip, but because it always seemed like I was having to give something up because "God said". I was getting tired and weary of always doing the right thing, but then the Lord refreshed me and led me to His Word in Mark 10:29-30 NIV where it says "'Truly, I tell you,' Jesus replied, 'no one who has left home or brothers or sisters or mother or father or children or fields for me and the gospel will fail to receive a hundred times as much in this present age: homes, brothers, sisters, mothers, children and fields – along with persecutions – an in the age to come eternal life."

What the Lord was saying is that yes, there is a cost for following me. There are some things and some people you will have to give up, but do not be discouraged because mark my word before you transition to eternity, in this life, I will see to it that you receive many times over whatever you had to give up. Keep in mind though, that these things will come with persecution because you are following me. Some people may think that it doesn't take all of that or you are doing the most, but stay focused. Oh, and on top of that, the icing on the cake is that you get eternal life after this life is all over.

I was so encouraged after reading those verses and letting God speak to my heart as it pertains to my specific situation. After that, I put on my big girl pants and began to believe that God would reward us for our obedience. It was not because He had to. It was because He is a good Father who loves and gives good gifts to His children, and because of what He had already spoken to me. I just knew He would.

Well, do you know that by the time our honeymoon came around we had 2 FREE plane tickets to St. Lucia worth over $2000?! In addition, our entire honeymoon was paid for without any trouble thanks to people sowing seeds and giving to our honeymoon registry. Can you guess what resort we stayed at for our honeymoon? It was a Sandals resort-yes the same resort brand John was awarded for President's Club that I had given up months prior. Our accommodations included a 5 night stay at a top-of-the-line villa with our own private plunge pool on the balcony AND personal butlers. And as if that was not enough, we were surprised with a candlelight dinner on the beach which was gifted to us as well as a private transfer from the resort to the airport. We went on excursions, a helicopter ride, went to the spa TWICE, and ate all the food our hearts desired. Not to mention I got to LEGALLY enjoy my HUSBAND. God is so so faithful and even if He didn't do any of those things I would still follow and obey Him because He is God, and He is good. Our acts of obedience have a far greater reward than what we could ever imagine.

The story doesn't end there though, it gets so much better. Remember that scripture I was standing on said one hundredfold. I guess all of that amazingness that we experienced on our honeymoon was not enough though. The very next year I, too was awarded President's Club with the company I worked for at the time, and what did I get? An all-inclusive trip to Hawaii, a place I had desired to go for the longest time! This trip could not have come at a better time either. Because I was pregnant with our daughter Isabella, this trip served as our babymoon. Listen, I cannot make this stuff up, God is just so so good. It pays to put our trust in Him and obey Him in every area.

The best part of this is the fact that through me sharing my experience with family, friends, and my networks on social media, so many people were inspired to continue or start on their journey of abstinence and honoring God in their body. Even if none of the trips ever happened, that alone would make it all worth it because, at the end of the day, this is all for the glory of God.

One of the best parts of knowing I honored God with my body by waiting is knowing that generational curses were broken in the process. There is now a new story in my bloodline. I am able to pass down a legacy of purity and obedience to my children and any future children. Even though I didn't know anyone who had ever done this before, God was my help. I was no saint. I had a past as do many people. No matter what you have done or where you find yourself right now, know that you too can write a new story and secure a new legacy.

How to Wait

Once you decide that you are going to honor God in this area, the great thing is that you can rely on God's strength and His grace to keep you. 2 Corinthians 12:9 declares that God's strength is made perfect in our weakness, so even though our flesh may be weak, we can always tap into God's strength and let it be perfected in and through us so that we can overcome. I believe that one of the reasons that many people fail in their pursuit of abstinence is because they are relying more on willpower than God's power. There is only so much willpower you can exercise before you just completely fail and end up indulging way more than you ever anticipated. Your willpower will only get you so far, but His power will take you all the way to your wedding day as well as sustain you in your marriage. Yes, the Bible tells us that we must exercise self-control (control of ourselves), but it also tells us that self-control is a fruit of the Spirit as outlined in

Galatians 5:22-23. This means that self-control (and any of the 9 fruit of the Spirit for that matter) will be exercised and manifested in you as a result of the Holy Spirit working in and through you.

So, how do you tap into that grace and power to keep you? Spending time in the presence of God through worship, prayer, reading, and listening to the Word or just soaking in His presence is the best way to do this. When you spend time with the Father, you just cannot remain the same. He begins to speak to you, affirm you, and manifest Himself to you in different ways all the while transforming you bit by bit without you even realizing at first. Another really powerful way to do this is by studying and meditating on God's Word concerning the area of holiness, purity, and abstaining from fornication and sexual immorality. I don't mean just read a few scriptures and be done with it. I mean really taking the time to study them out, write them down, journal them, speak them out loud over and over again, confess them over yourself, and whatever else you have to do to get them rooted and grounded in your heart. The Word works and is full of power, but the reason why so many Christians are not seeing that power manifested in their life is because they are too shallow with their Word. You have to dig deep so that you are getting the revelation for yourself and it becomes more than just words in a book or on your iPhone. The Bible is clear, For the word of God is living and powerful, and sharper than any two-edged sword, piercing even to the division of soul and spirit, and of joints and marrow, and is a discerner of the thoughts and intents of the heart (Hebrews 4:12).

Guard Your Heart

We already talked about guarding your heart in the process of getting over a breakup, but it is also important in your abstinence journey. As

I stated before, I am still very passionate and very intentional about guarding my heart even while married, and I believe that it is one of the things that helped me the most while I was in my season of waiting. Not only did it help me to keep my body, but it also helped me to not get anxious about being in a relationship or being married.

Remember, Proverbs 4:23 NLT says, "Guard your heart above all else, for it determines the course of your life." The word heart here refers to your innermost being, your spirit, that place which is the very seat of your will and emotions. When you guard something, this means you are protecting it by putting a barrier or restriction of some sort over it. What this verse is saying is that you have to protect what you are letting into your very core. Well, how do things get into our hearts since the heart is a part of our inner being? We let them in through our physical senses-mainly our ears and our eyes. This is why when I was single I did not listen to any secular music, even R&B, and love songs. Remember 1 Corinthians 10:23 KJV says, "All things are lawful for me, but all things are not expedient. All things are lawful for me, but all things edify not." In other words, what Paul was saying is that even though something may be permissible, it does not mean that you should do it. Not everything that is allowed is going to be beneficial to get you where you are trying to go in life.

When we listen to certain songs, it puts us in certain moods. Music is extremely powerful in that way. Certain ideas and feelings are being subconsciously fed into our spirit or our 'heart", and we know that whatever we feed on will eventually affect our life because it has to come out. That is why we can get into certain moods and in our feelings and not even understand why sometimes.

Back then, I would also (and still do) limit what I watch on TV and carefully monitor my social media feed and use. It's also important to be careful about what we are reading because the things that seem the most harmless could be having the biggest effect on us. For example, I used to love to binge on romantic comedies and read romance novels all the while subconsciously fantasizing about my future love life. We have to understand that all of these mediums are constantly feeding us images and ideas and we are just eating it up. Not to mention, those storylines are nothing like real life, and so they are also selling us false expectations. Most people would call me extreme and say that I am doing the most, but you do not get the God kind of results by doing what everyone else is doing. You get the God kind of results by doing what God says (in His Word and when He speaks to you individually) even if it seems strange or extreme, and even if everyone else does not agree. Proverbs was clear. It says, whatever you let into your heart determines the course of your life. Eventually, the fruit of your life and the harvest thereof will look like the seeds that have been planted in your heart through all these mediums of influence. Make a decision that you are going to be a good steward over your heart by fiercely and diligently protecting it against all that the world tries to plant into it.

While you don't want to fill your spirit with just any old garbage, you also do not want to sit around bored and idle. Have you ever heard the saying: An idle mind is the devil's playground?" Well, it's true. Matthew 12: 43-45 KJV illustrates this. It says, "When the unclean spirit is gone out of a man, he walketh through dry places, seeking rest, and findeth none. Then he saith, I will return unto my house from whence I came out; and when he is come, he findeth it empty, swept and garnished." Then he goes and takes with him seven other spirits more wicked than himself, and they enter and dwell there, and the last state of that man is worse than the first. "If you're not filling yourself with anything at all, and you are just empty like what the scripture illustrated, you are leaving yourself susceptible to the enemy's wiles.

He may try to play all types of tricks in your head such as confusion, depression, or hopelessness. You can begin to feel lonely, your mind can start wandering, and the enemy can begin to play tricks on your mind. Therefore, you must be intentional about feeding your spirit good things. Meditate on the Word and other things that are going to elevate your spirit and your life. We want everything that we let into our hearts to be edifying. Like I mentioned before, The Word holds all the power, so it is the best place to start. Reading good books, watching quality programming, and listening to edifying music is also good.

Accountability

We talked a bit about accountability earlier with regards to growing in your relationship with God. It is also vitally important on your quest for sexual purity. We all need someone, and if we know that someone else is holding us accountable for our actions, then we are more likely to follow through with what we said we were going to do. Ideally, this would be a person who is on the same journey with you so that you all can feed off of each other and you understand each other. When one of you is weak, the other can be strong, and you can help push each other to be better. If not, a mentor or someone you look up to will also work.

Watch out for distractions

Once you decide that you are going to save yourself for marriage please believe that the enemy is not going to like it. He will send distractions in the form of a man who is NOT YOUR HUSBAND. He is a counterfeit, and you will know it because he will not be on the same page as you and your journey. Walk away, and do not open a door for that kind of temptation. If you are quick to swerve all the fakes, it will make the journey to your real husband come quicker. I know this because I have been there.

After I decided to not date for the sake of dating, the enemy had to switch up his tactics for presenting guys to me. He now knew that I was not going to settle for just anyone, so he sent me that guy who told me that God said I am his wife. This guy came to church with me, claimed to love God, and wanted to marry me, but I should have known he was not the one because he was constantly leading me to his bedroom. I came so close to breaking my abstinence promise to God with this guy on several occasions until I finally had to put my foot down and end the relationship. Learn from my mistakes, don't let it get that far, and don't fall for every piece of bait Satan tries to trap you with.

The Real Test

When you do get into a relationship, the real tests will come. It is much easier to abstain when you're not talking to anyone because there are no real opportunities for temptation. So, when you get into a relationship, set boundaries. Be honest with yourself. I don't care how holy or how "strong" we claim to be. We are all human and we have fleshly desires. When you are in a relationship, then apparently you are attracted to that person, and so you don't want to find yourself in any compromising situations. Maybe you have to limit or eliminate any physical touch such as hugging or kissing. Maybe it's not a good idea for the two of you to be alone. Whatever your boundaries are, just be honest and don't try to bring fire to your bosom and expect not to get burned. (Proverbs 6:27).

Dispelling the Fear

Whenever I used to tell people that I was waiting for marriage to have sex again, I would get a range of responses. Most of the time though, people would try to project their fears onto me. They would say things like "What if the sex is bad?" or "You will never find a man who would be willing to do that" or "My boyfriend will never go for that." Listen, sis, if you don't understand anything else that I say to you in this book, hear this: God is GOOD. Why would a good God give a bad gift to His children? Matthew 7:11 NIV says this, "If you then, being evil, know how to give good gifts to your children, how much more will your Father who is in heaven give good things to those who ask Him!" Why would God make you wait all of that time to abstain from sex only to let it be bad? I don't know about you, but that is just not the kind of God that I serve. Remember I spoke about how He honors us when we honor Him? You have to have faith and trust that God always has your best interest in mind and cares about every single detail of your life and your marriage.

I understand your rationale if you feel like you are not going to be able to find someone willing to wait for you. I know the statistics are not in your favor when you think about the ratio of women to men. Then add on the ratio of Christian women to Christian men and the odds seem even more bleak. Then add the ratio of Christian women to Christian men who are willing to wait for marriage to be intimate with you and your chances seem like one in a million. Then add on all of the other details like must not be crazy, must be financially stable, etc. etc. and you probably find it hard to believe that you are ever going to find true love at all. Listen, don't get caught up in all of those details. My God is not a God who is moved by the statistics of this world. If you get to thinking like that then that means you do not trust Him like you say you do. Thank God it doesn't take a million men anyway, you only need one.

As far as you being worried that your little boyfriend will never go for you wanting to abstain from sex, it may be time for you to give that relationship up sis. No man should be the determining factor in what you do with your body. You should desire to obey God above all, not appease some guy who does not respect or protect your purity. If you are going to succeed in your journey of keeping yourself until marriage, then you are going to have to take responsibility for your own purity. You cannot expect a man or anyone else to do that for you. No matter how much they claim to love you, they are human and they have their desires and temptations just like you do. This is why it is so important for you to make your purity a priority and be diligent in taking the proper measures and setting appropriate boundaries for yourself.

Despite what seems to be popular today and despite what the rest of the world is doing. Despite what society may deem as normal, and despite what people may try to convince you of otherwise, God has not changed His mind about this subject. He still expects and respects holiness, and He would not ask something of us that He knew we could not do. Trust Him in this walk. It. can. be. Done. If you want it. I am a living witness and so are countless other individuals. It's just not popular or what you see in the media, so you may think that no one is doing it anymore, but that is a lie. It does not matter what your past is, you can decide today that you are going to honor God and your future spouse and save yourself for marriage.

CHAPTER 8

Submission- not for the faint at heart

What is it about the word submission that makes us cringe as soon as we hear it? When we hear submission, we automatically think weak, subservient, inferior, pushover, and several other terms that are in no way appealing. However, that is in no way what submission is all about. Whether we realize it or not, we are all submitted to someone if not, several someone's. Think about it. We are submitted to our parents until we reach a certain age or go out on our own. We are submitted to our boss if we work for a company. We are submitted to the government as citizens of the country we live in. Submission is required for any type of system and institution to work and the institution of marriage is no different. Ephesians 5: 22-24 KJV says this: "Wives, submit yourselves to your own husbands as you do to the Lord. For the husband is the head of the wife as Christ is the head of the church, his body, of which he is the Savior. Now as the church submits to Christ, so also wives should submit to their husbands in everything."

The reason He gives us an order is so that everything can run smoothly. If there is a differing of opinions somewhere, there has to be someone who has the final say otherwise nothing will ever be accomplished. I have found that God doesn't give us rules, commands, and orders to be cruel. Instead, He gives them to us for our good so that we may be successful and get things accomplished. If we were too busy worrying about whose decision should be the one to prevail, nothing would ever be accomplished. For these reasons, submission is one of those things that you are going to need in order to be found and stay found. So, I'd like to peel back the layers on this topic to bring forth some clarity.

Submission in Relationships

For years, I wore the strong independent woman title with pride. I grew up way before my time and eventually I learned to do everything for myself, by myself and I didn't need anyone's help. In one sense there isn't anything wrong with that. It is a beautiful thing when someone beats the odds and accomplishes certain things in life despite the hand life dealt them. The single mom who worked her way through school and works hard to provide for her family. The underprivileged child who grew up and became the first person in her family to graduate from college. The lady who was raised with no father or male figures but turned out just fine in spite of. The person who wanted to be the complete opposite of what they saw around them so they worked extra hard to make something of themself. Whatever your narrative, it is to be commended. But sometimes we can unknowingly rob ourselves of the beautiful freedom that comes with being equally yoked with a real man.

A man that will lead us, cover us, make plans, think ahead, take charge, provide and protect. The issue is sometimes we can sabotage a good thing before it even begins. We've resorted to letting Instagram memes tell us how we should conduct ourselves in a relationship or on our journey to finding one. We know you're a boss, that you're independent, and you're making things happen, but that does not take away from the fact that you need to be loved, protected, and cherished and a man needs to feel needed, be respected, and treated like the leader he is.

I know what you're thinking "Rita, a real man should be able to handle all of this." And to that, I would say: a real man should not and will not compete for a position in a relationship that is rightfully his. Furthermore, anything with two heads will constantly be at odds with one another. Eventually, the rest of the body (marriage) will die if the two heads keep butting with each other.

But I feel you. I knew that in a marriage, the Bible calls us to submit one to another and calls the husband the head; so, I desired to give my husband a submissive wife. However, that did not and still does not always prove to be the easiest thing to do. Like many things, it is easier said than done. I remember being on the phone with John one day while we were dating and having a casual conversation. I must have asked him about something but then went on to offer several more options because all of a sudden he stopped me and asked "Why did you ask me for my opinion if you weren't going to accept it?". I wish I could remember the specifics of the conversation, but I don't. The only thing I remember is being taken aback because I didn't see myself as doing anything wrong; I was only doing what I had always done which is analyzing a situation and trying to figure it out all by myself. I didn't realize that by doing that it felt as if I did not value his decision-making skills or his opinion. After all, I just disregarded it and was going to keep it moving. See, sometimes it's not even a blatant rebellion that we display. Sometimes it can be in the subtle things we do and say. So, the main thing to adjust is your attitude concerning this entire topic.

As with many things, submission is an attitude of the heart so whatever is going on in there manifests in your actions. As long as you have the correct attitude, your actions will begin to follow if you put some effort behind it and work on it. It will certainly require a renewing of the mind. We renew our minds by reading and rereading God's Word concerning a particular subject. What does the Bible have to say about submission in marriage? Meditate on it, and allow God to work on you from the inside out. He specializes in heart changes, and He will grace you.

I know what else you're thinking, "Rita this man is not my husband, so I do not need to submit to him right now." And to that, I would say you are absolutely correct. You are not required to submit to any man who is not your husband. However, when it comes to submission - there are levels to this- meaning a boyfriend is not going to get the same level of submission as a fiance' and a fiance' is not going to get the same level of submission as a husband, but there should be some sort of submitting at each level. There is not going to be some sort of switch that goes off in your brain the day you say "I do" which instantly makes you a submissive wife. This is something that you want you to begin "practicing" for lack of a better word right now. Besides, how will your mate know you are even capable of submitting if you wait until the wedding day? Chances are you will never make it there if he doesn't see it in you before then.

While John and I were dating, I would yield to him in certain situations. For example, I used to be very strong-willed when it comes to doing my own thing. I had been single for a while and I was used to doing things my way. John didn't like it when I would do things such as go to the ATM or the gas station late at night by myself or just small things that I didn't see as a big deal because again I had been doing it my way for so long. Instead of continuing to go back and forth with him, I decided to just listen to him, and slowly but surely, he began to chip away at my stubbornness. When we got engaged, I took it a step further. I let him have the final say when it came to some of the decisions, even ones that did not directly affect our future together. I was getting myself into the mindset of letting him lead as well as showing him that I was capable of letting him do so.

Now, notice I said there is a beautiful freedom that comes with being EQUALLY yoked to a REAL MAN. If you are trying to do this with a man who does not fit into both of those categories (equally yoked and REAL MAN) then you will find yourself frustrated and fighting the process. You have to be able to trust the person who is leading you, otherwise, you will never be able to fully let go trust, and submit. The reason why it is so easy to submit to John is that I know that he is fully submitted to God. That fact puts my mind at ease knowing that I am covered by my husband and we both are covered by Christ. There are men who will make the submission process frustrating and others who will make it easy. A man who is truly submitted to God will make it easy because that means he takes his cues from God. This also means he is less likely to abuse his privileges. He will respect your opinion and include you in the decision-making process. He will not lead with misogyny or chauvinism but in tender love and care knowing that he is leading you both back to Christ, not himself.

To be completely honest, it feels good to follow my husband's lead as He submits to Christ. It feels as if a huge weight was lifted off of my shoulders, a weight that I now know was a part chip and part weight of the world that I carried. Leave it up to us women, especially us black women to always feel like we have to carry some sort of burden because that's just what we do, we always make it happen. But can I free you really quickly? Just because you CAN, does not mean that you have to. See, we were never meant to carry such a load in the first place- we weren't built for it, and that's why some of us are breaking down. We watched mama, big mama, and many generations of women who came before us just do what they have to do and keep it moving, but that does not have to be your story. Allow yourself the chance to experience the beautiful freedom that comes with being equally yoked to a real man.

Submission Does Not Begin and End in Marriage

To be honest, my attitude towards submission began to change way before I began dating my husband. My attitude and actions towards submission were being changed the minute I decided to dedicate my life to Christ. As I sat under my pastor in church, I decided I would be submitted to that ministry and covering. As I served in different areas of the church, I decided I would submit to whatever leader was in the department. As God began to give me godly friends who I could trust, I decided I would submit myself to their accountability. The reason why it became easier to submit in these areas, however, is that I had finally submitted myself to God. Submission, much like everything else in life, begins and ends with God.

Before committing myself to God, I had a rebellious heart. I did whatever I wanted to do whenever I wanted to do it, and I didn't feel the need to answer to anyone. But once I became fully committed to God in my thoughts, heart, and actions, it made submitting to everything and everyone else easy. I was able to fully wrap my head around what it means to lay down my selfish desires and motives through my relationship with God. "Not my will, but your will be done" became my heart's pursuit. If you are struggling with submission in any form or at any level, I challenge you to take a look at your relationship with God first. Can you truly say that you are submitted to Him in EVERY area of your life? Yes, you may be submitted to Him in the area of sexual purity but are you submitted to Him in your career/life aspirations? Yeah, you may be submitted to Him in your giving, but are you submitted to Him when it comes to your love life? I've found there's usually an area or two that we are not fully submitted in, an area we have not completely let God have full reign over. If He were to tell us to go one way, we would probably still go in the opposite direction. If you're not sure, pray and ask God to show you any area where you are not fully submitted to Him, and that will help lead you to full submission in other relationships in your life.

Much of submitting has a lot to do with humility. Humility is the opposite of pride. When we are humble, we don't make it all about us. Instead, we can step outside of ourselves for a greater purpose. I don't think that it is a coincidence that right after Peter admonished the younger people to submit to the elders in 1 Peter 5, that he then followed it up with "be clothed in humility". Take a look: *Likewise you younger people, submit yourselves to your elders. Yes, all of you be submissive to one another, and be clothed with humility, for "God resists the proud, but gives grace to the humble." Therefore humble yourselves under the mighty hand of God, that He may exalt you in due time. -1 Peter 5: 5-6*

From these passages, we can gather that submission and humility go hand in hand. It takes a humble person to be submissive. be prideful; You can't submit yourself to a friend or accountability partner and it just will not work. The minute they call you out about something or admonish you concerning a situation, you are more than likely going to get defensive or brush it off. You can't submit yourself to a department in a church to serve and be prideful. Because the minute they do something, plan something, or operate in a way that you don't necessarily agree with, you may get offended or even want to quit. You can't submit yourself to a husband and be prideful and make it work. Because as soon as they make a decision for the family you don't agree with you'll probably make it all about you. Are you picking up what I'm putting down?

What does submission look like outside of the context of romantic relationships? It looks like not getting an attitude when leadership says or does something that you don't necessarily agree with on the team where you serve. It looks like continuing to serve as unto the Lord. It looks like being open when friends try to tell you something about your character that you may not see but they do, instead of thinking that they're "hating" on you or overreacting. It looks like humbling yourself and taking your cues from other people sometimes, as opposed to always having to be the one to call the shots.

Like many other things in this Christian walk and marriage, you cannot conquer the area of submission on your own. You will need God's grace (his supernatural enablement and empowerment) for you to be successful. Remember, it's not submission if you agree. Submission kicks in when you do not necessarily agree with the other person's stance, yet you decide to cooperate and submit yourself to their decision anyway, regardless of the implications. The great thing about God is even if the other person is wrong, because you honored that person through your submission you also honored God and therefore God will cover both of you. There is protection in submitting and operating in God's order. He will make sure that everything works out for your good. Trust Him in the area of submission.

PART IV

THE CONCLUSION

C H A P T E R   9

Practical Preparation

Remember the guy who broke up with me? The one who gave me my first (and hopefully only) heartbreak? Well, several months after he had broken up with me, my phone rang, and it was him on the other end of the call. I was just beginning to feel a little relief from the pain. Yet, here he was calling my phone to "check on me" after breaking up with me just months prior. The sting of the breakup wasn't so bad anymore; so I entertained his conversation and chatted for just a few minutes. Towards the end of the call, he hit me with a very poignant question: "What have you learned," he asked. What have I learned? WHAT HAVE I LEARNED? Dude, you courted me for months and sold me dreams about our future together. You made me fall for you only to break up with me in the end. Yet, you have the audacity to ask ME what have I learned? Where they do that at???

That's what I wanted to say, but I didn't. I knew exactly what he was asking me. Behind those four words were much more substance than the novice Rita would have even recognized. But the much more mature Rita of that time knew and understood the depth of the question. So as much as I wanted to roll my eyes and turn the question on him, I didn't. Instead, I started to run down the list of things I had learned over the past several months. I didn't even necessarily seek to learn these things, but somewhere in the process of healing came a lot of prayer which begot introspection which begot wisdom which begot total healing and restoration. What he was trying to figure out is if I had grown any during our time apart. Did I realize and recognize my mistakes and shortcoming in the relationship or was I still going to blame the break-up completely on him because he's the one that pulled the proverbial plug on the relationship?

I clearly recall being in relationships thinking that the person I was in a relationship with was so blessed to have me as their significant other, but now that I look back with fresh eyes, I'm seriously trying to figure out what is it that I was bringing to the table? That is besides what any other nice-looking, relatively intellectual woman could bring. I mean don't get me wrong. I am well-educated, I know how to hold a good conversation, and I am a great listener among other things, but so are millions of other women. At the end of the day what made me think that I was capable of being someone's wife? The truth is that back then I did not know the first thing about being someone's wife, yet there I was coveting the title.

At some point, you have to have an honest conversation with yourself and analyze what exactly you are bringing to the table. A marriage is a partnership and like any partnership, it is only as strong as its weakest member. You must think about what you have to offer to another person and superficial things will not cut it. Many times, as women we have an entire list of things we want in a man. We want him to have some class about himself but at the same time have a little edge. We want him to be funny, mature, honest, faithful and have a good career. We want him to be tall, charismatic, have a sixpack, and all this other stuff we throw out there. Yet, we are nowhere near those things ourselves. I know you have some sort of list, just like I had at many points in my singleness. You know the one where we take either mental or physical note of all of our partner desirables? Choose today that you are going to be the standard before you project the standard. Decide that you are going to become before you expect someone to be your list. I am in no way saying throw away your standards, desires, and expectations. I am simply stating that your time would be better served working on YOU.

Remember our scripture from the beginning of the book, Proverbs 18:22? He who finds a wife, finds a GOOD THING and obtains favor from the Lord. Remember that wife is the state in which your future husband will find you, not something that you will magically become when he puts a ring on your finger the day of your wedding. Remember, being a wife is a posture of the heart and is manifested in your actions before you even say I do. There are some things you are going to want to work on in the natural if you desire to be a godly wife. Now is the time to prepare. Now is the time to carry yourself as such.

Titus 2:5 gives us guidelines for a godly wife stating that wives should be "discreet, chaste, homemakers, good, obedient to their own husbands, that the word of God may not be blasphemed". I want to outline a few questions you may want to ask yourself based on this passage. Keep in mind this is not the end all be all. However, it is a very good starting place.

1. **Are you submissive?**

    We just took an entire chapter to discuss submission, so I will only point out one more thing. The two people in a marriage are actually submitted one to another (Ephesians 5:21) but the man is the head of the woman and Christ is the head of him (Ephesians 5:23). There is a reason God has this divine order. There is a covering and safety attached to this setup. Will submission be easy? Not always. Especially if you are a Type A personality like me. Submission says I will do it your way because I honor and respect you and God's way of doing things. The good news is that even if the man gets it wrong or misses it, you are still covered and protected by God Almighty because you were in the right ORDER if you listened and submitted to your man. No man wants a quarrelsome, rebellious, nagging wife. Proverbs 27:15 says that a quarrelsome wife is as annoying as a constant dripping on a rainy day. Don't be that woman. You want to make the atmosphere of your home one of peace that your man looks forward to coming home to at the end of the day, not one that he avoids and looks to other people, places, and things to seek solace.

2. **Are you domestic?**

    Ok, let me stop trying to be all politically correct. Woman, can you cook, clean, and keep up a home? Yes, I know this is the 21st century and women are good for way more than doing things in the home. I also understand that times have changed, and many women are out here making power moves in all different sectors of society. Trust me, I'm here for it. In fact, I consider myself to be one of those women. However, none of that negates the fact that a wife is to be the keeper of her home (according to Titus 2).

Listen, no real man wants a woman who does not keep a clean house and does not know how to cook a decent meal. Even if he doesn't say it, trust me, he's thinking it. I am not saying that you have to be Suzy Homemaker or Martha Stewart, but you must realize that as a woman and the keeper of the house, you are responsible for making sure your home is in order. This doesn't mean that you have to do everything yourself either. If we take a close look at the Proverbs 31 woman, we will realize that even she had help. Proverbs 31:15 says this: She also rises while it is yet night, and provides food for her household, and a portion for her maidservants. That's right. This wife, mother, businesswoman, and some would even say the epitome of biblical womanhood was no doubt a girl boss, but even she had maids. See, being the keeper of your home doesn't mean that you have to do it all yourself. However, it does mean that you oversee all the details, and you are the one chiefly responsible for the state of your home including your home's atmosphere. Proverbs 31:27 says, "she watches the ways of her household." I love that verse. It lets me know that nothing should get past me in my home. I like to consider myself the project manager of it all, and I take my role very seriously. This means that I make sure that my husband and children are eating the right things to keep us all in optimal health. I am responsible for making sure my children are being nurtured, cared for, and learning well. I am responsible for making sure our home is a clean, inviting space for everyone to live in. I am responsible for making sure my husband has everything he needs to walk out all of his assignments. I can go on and on. The list is endless. Any good project manager knows, however, that some things must be outsourced. There is nothing wrong with a housekeeper, a chef, a nanny, a personal trainer, a meal prep service, or anything else that you may need to keep your household running. The important thing is that you are making your home a priority and not putting any ministry, career, business, or anything else in front of that.

All of these are things you can begin learning and putting into practice now. Again, this is not something that you want to just start exploring once you say I do. Instead, practice while you are still single. Some practical things that you can do to begin building good habits include being diligent about keeping your house clean and not letting things pile up before you decide to tidy up as well as learning how to cook a few decent meals and have some staple recipes that you can pull out in a clutch. There are too many tools at your disposal for you to not even know how to boil water: Pinterest, those Tasty Facebook videos, YouTube, and meal delivery services such as Hello Fresh just to name a few. Now, not later, is the time to begin molding yourself into that Proverbs 31 woman we all love to quote.

3. **Do you have a servant's heart?**
    One of the biggest things you are going to have to let go of to have a successful marriage is selfishness. A selfish or self-absorbed person is constantly concerned about me, me, me or self, self, self. A selfless person is more concerned about how they can serve the other person. Most of the time we're concerned about what the other person can do for us instead of what we can do for them. Many times, our selfishness is

not even apparent, and it can be hard for us to see it. I bet you're already thinking to yourself how there's no way being selfish even applies to you. Well, when you get into a marriage and you begin to share your life, your space, and your entire world with someone else, all of your selfish tendencies are exposed and become evident. This is especially true if you have been single for a long time because you are so used to doing everything your way, living a certain way, and being concerned about yourself only because it has been that way for so long. Now is the time to start taking inventory of these things and making adjustments in your mindset and your actions so that you are not blind-sided once the honeymoon is over. Being a spouse is all about how you can meet the other person's needs, and it is no longer all about you. Now, IT IS your spouse's job to be concerned with meeting your needs but let's be honest, sometimes it will seem as if things are a little one-sided because the other person is not going to keep up their end of the bargain 100 percent of the time. The truth is, we all miss the mark sometimes. But, that does not give you a free pass to let up on your serving the other person. It is certainly easier said than done but you must learn to depend on God to meet your every need because humans will always fall short of perfection.

A good way to get some good experience in this area is by serving at your home church. Serving and getting plugged in at church is often overlooked but it is so very important. Being planted and serving at your local church puts you in position to be found. Does this mean that your husband is someone in your church? I am not saying that. He may be but then again he may not be. What I am saying is that being planted in a church puts you in position to be found as well as puts you in a position to carry out your God-given purpose. If God places and plants you somewhere that means He has something just for you right there at that place under those pastors and that leadership.

To my point, when you serve, you begin to focus on the needs of others without even considering yourself or expecting anything in return. You begin using your gifts, talents, and your time to glorify God and advance His kingdom. Many times, you have to be to church early and leave late. Sometimes you have to come to church on days other people do not have to. Sometimes you encounter and have to love people who aren't so loveable (and all the ushers said...Amen). And you are doing all of this without getting paid. There are no real incentives. Serving comes from a selfless place within you. That is why it is such a great training ground for marriage and any other relationship.

You can also start practicing servanthood in your current familial relationships and friendships. Try to be more mindful of opportunities to serve the other person and make it about them rather than yourself. Some of you don't even like sharing your food. Come on now. Be free from the "it's all about me" attitude because that is one of the quickest ways to bring down any relationship.

4. **Do you have a prayer life?**

I will probably mention prayer every chance I get. Why? Because my public life is a living, breathing manifestation of private time in prayer (among other things) but mainly prayer. I think that prayer is one of those things that we take for granted or unconsciously belittle. We tend to use it as a last resort instead of going to it first. And even if we do pray, we still try to do things in our own power, overriding what we prayed. Ok, I'm off my soapbox but my point is you will most definitely need a prayer life in marriage more than ever because most of your battles will be won on your knees. So many women try to change their spouse or try to get him to see things their way not realizing that we cannot change a man. Only God can work on a person's heart causing them to change. We can talk to our man until we are blue in the face, give examples, pie charts, statistics, graphs, and the whole nine and he still will not understand. Let me give you a quick example of this.

I tried to change John early on in our courtship, and it did not go over very well. It was the catalyst behind our very first "real" argument. I was unhappy because he was used to being friendly and chatty with members of the opposite sex, so naturally, he didn't stop once we got together. I confronted him about his "friendliness" and he hit me with the "you're trying to change me" line. This was despite all of my attempts to explain to him that there is a way people behave when they are single and a way they operate when they have the intentions of marrying someone, and the two are very different. Even though he saw his behavior as harmless and didn't mean anything by it, I knew that some women would take it a different way. After much communicating back and forth about the issue, it seemed we had hit an impasse. So, I did what I knew to do about any situation I have no control over, I prayed.

I didn't pray from a place of "Lord you better get your son because he is tripping, and I need him to understand where

I am coming from." You know how we like to do. Instead, I prayed that if there was something that I needed to do differently in the situation or if there was a mindset change that I needed to have then I asked God to enlighten me. Then I prayed that God would rectify the entire situation and give us the solution we needed since neither one of us seemed to be budging. I came out of that prayer session with so much peace, and I got the sense that I should not mention my concerns to John anymore. Well, do you know that not even a week had gone by before John came to me with this sudden "new revelation" about how he should be operating differently since he was moving away from singleness and that he would start adjusting the way he interacts with other women? He was pretty much telling me everything that I was trying to convey to him that day during our conversation, but for some reason, he didn't get it back then. Do you know why that is? Because it wasn't my job to try to change him.

There is a difference between information and revelation. I was feeding him information when I was trying to get him to see things my way. But God knew how to speak to John the way he needed to hear it and was able to give him a revelation. Besides, I didn't want him thinking he had to change who he was for me. Remember, anything a person does for another human being will not last. It has to be their idea for them to exhibit any real change. I never had that issue with John being too friendly or too chatty with the opposite sex ever again. I would even joke sometimes that his behavior comes off as a little rude because he always tries to honor me in that area whether I'm around or not. When the change comes as a result of a person's own personal revelation, the results will be lasting.

If anyone changes because you told them to, chances are the results will only be temporary. All

of this came as a result of prayer. Instead of trying to change the situation in the natural, I used my spiritual weapon of prayer which was a spiritual discipline I learned to develop and cultivate while I was single.

Prayer is your weapon in every situation, but especially in marriage. You will have to know how to pray for your husband and your marriage in general because Satan comes to attack unions, especially godly ones.

How are you supposed to undergird your husband in prayer if you are still struggling to get up in the mornings and pray over your day? Sis, your role as a wife will be imperative to the growth, strength, spiritual life, and success of your husband (just to name a few). If you're struggling to get up and spend time with God today, it is not going to get easier to pray when you are married. It gets a bit more challenging because you have so much more on your plate. No one is perfect. God isn't seeking someone to check something off of their to-do list for the day, but He is looking for you to get a good foundation now. You are called to be his helpmeet, keeper of your home, his rib (protecting his most delicate places) and so much more. Do you know that as a wife you will have more authority in prayer for him than any other person? It's important to learn how to pray, cultivate, and maintain your time with God now so that you will have no problems later when you are someone's wife.

You should also begin praying for your husband now even though you probably do not know who he is. I was as single as can be with no prospect in sight, but I knew that I was called to be a wife. I would periodically pray for the man who I was called to. I would pray that God would give him a spirit of wisdom and revelation in the knowledge of Him (Ephesians 1), that he was growing in the Word and his relationship with God, and that everything he puts his hands to would prosper (among other things depending on how I was led). Do you know that when I finally started dating John, he would tell me about everything that was going on in his life at the time and he would mention how that past year he had grown in his relationship with God more than ever in his life, he was prospering at work more than ever and so on and so on? God was literally answering my prayers before I even knew the WHO. I would suggest praying how you are led for your future mate. God may have work to do in your husband before he finds you just like He is doing work in you.

5. **Are you modest in behavior and appearance?** Ok, so I am going to tell on myself for a second here. Years ago (B.C.) when I was feeling a little lonely or like no one was checking for me I would snap a picture of myself in the mirror with a tight or short outfit on with a sexy face and post it to social media. This was before front-facing cameras were a thing. Keep in mind, I wanted to be a wife or at the very least in a decent relationship with a man of substance, but yet I was trying to attract a guy by exposing my body. Hmmm. What's wrong with that picture? So, I wanted a man of a certain caliber, and I eventually wanted to be someone's wife yet what I was doing was only going to attract a certain type of man, and it was not the type of man I said I wanted. All that type of behavior is going to get you is a whole bunch of likes from the wrong type

of people and annoying D.M's to your inbox from men who don't have a faithful, committed bone in their body.

But Rita men are visual and how else would he know what I'm working with if I don't show him? Yes, men are visual, but do you honestly think that the type of man that you say you want would want his lady flaunting their goods on the internet? No ma'am. Usually, as women, if we feel the need to behave that way there is an underlying issue we need to deal with. My advice is to get to the root of it and find out what's going on in your heart. Is it insecurity, loneliness, low self-esteem, attention-seeking? The man God has for you will SEE you for who you are. He will see you whether you're wearing a garbage bag or a skimpy outfit. You don't need to try to capture his attention and you certainly will not need to try to convince him of your worth. The right man will see you and see his rib not a pair of breasts or thighs. Don't misunderstand me, you should make yourself look attractive. Men are still visual. But that does not mean you are to make yourself look desperate.

Proverbs 12:4 states A wife of noble character is her husband's crown, but a disgraceful wife is like decay in his bones. So, I want you to shift your mentality. I want you to go around thinking, talking, walking, and acting like you are already someone's wife even if you have no clue who your husband is yet. You are his crown. You represent him, and I'm sure the right man wouldn't want his woman speaking a certain way, dressing a certain way, frequenting certain places, and acting a certain way. Perhaps you keep attracting the wrong type of man because of what you are putting out there, I was there before. Praise God it is not too late to make adjustments.

I now realize that many of the things mentioned in Titus 2 are things that God was cultivating in me before I was able to say that I was ready to be someone's wife. I hope that what we have covered here in this book gets the wheels spinning in your head and at the very least, leads to introspection. Am I saying that you have to go into marriage as a perfect person? Absolutely not. I am not saying that you have to have it all together because there is another level of growth and maturity that takes place after the vows. We never stop growing, and there is no way to fully prepare for marriage. However, it would behoove you to equip yourself through the study of the Word regarding what it means to be a godly wife. It is important to groom yourself with the help of the Holy Spirit and put yourself in the best position possible so that you can have the best marriage possible. Remember the book Act Like a Lady, Think Like a Man? Well, Steve Harvey may have been onto something. I've actually never read the book and probably wouldn't agree with all of his philosophy but THINKING a certain way certainly does affect your life. Proverbs 23:7 says "As a [wo]man thinks in his [her] heart so is [s]he". In other words, whatever you begin to think about yourself in those deep places of your heart, that's what behavior you will begin to exhibit. I challenge you to begin thinking like a wife and preparing to be one and watch what will begin to manifest in your life.

Closing Thoughts

Almost a decade has passed since that quarter-life crisis I spoke of in my introduction. Yet, I am still in awe of the transformation my life has experienced. I often sit in silence and just wonder at the goodness of God because most days it still feels surreal. To go from that to this. From there to here. From not much to exceeding abundantly above all I could ask, think or imagine just like Ephesians 3:20 describes.

It seems only fitting that I share with others that which the Lord has shared with me through His Word, revelations, and personal experiences. My hope and prayer is that you too would go from this to that and from here to there. Whatever this, that, here and there represents for you. That same Ephesians 3:20 God has a path and plan for your life too. Jeremiah 29:11 lets us know that it is not just any plan, but it is a good plan.

To some, it may seem odd that I encourage women to hide themselves in Christ. "Why would I choose to be hidden when I want to be found?" some ask. But the mystery of God is that as you hide yourself in Him, that is ironically where you find your life. Your true life. Not the one that you have tried to build for yourself. But the one He had planned for you all along, built on the Rock of your salvation. Keep your focus on Him, not the marriage, husband, or relationship. But on Him. Everything else will follow.

If you have made it this far in the book, it is likely that you are feeling one of two feelings: empowered or overwhelmed. You are either walking away feeling like you're pretty prepared and already on the right track or feeling like you have a lot of work to do. No matter which category you file yourself under, I want you to know an important fact. You are worthy right now. You are worthy of true love. You are worthy of your heart's desire. You are worthy of a good and godly man. You are worthy of a loving marriage. You are worthy of a love so deep that it makes you forget about every hurt, rejection, and disappointment of your past. You were worthy before you started reading this book and you will be worthy whether or not you implement a single principle. That is because your worthiness is not dependent on your readiness. You are worthy simply because God says you are. This book was written so that you would simply be ready for what you are already worthy of.

About Hidden & Found

Hidden & Found began as a blog Rita was led to start right after getting married. Now more than 4 years later, it is much more than that. It is a women's empowerment platform where Rita Brooks is afforded the opportunity to impact women all over the world. Hidden & Found ultimately exists to help women grow and remain grounded in their relationship with Christ. It also helps single women prepare and position themselves for a godly marriage, and it helps engaged and married women flourish in their unions. You can learn more about the ministry on Rita's website www.rita-brooks.com or on Instagram @hiddenandfound.

Closing Testimony

Hidden and Found literally found me when I was at a place of transition in my life. God had been recently revealing some things to me about myself that I was having a hard time sorting out, and putting into action. The day Hidden and Found requested to follow me on IG, I had literally been sitting in my car, on the way to church with tears in my eyes as God convicted me about some areas in my life that needed some adjusting. I accepted the request and read almost every blog within eyesight, and it was as if God was showing me how my life was and what it had the potential to be if I would obey, trust, and submit to him. I reached out to Rita, asking her advice on a particular subject, and the advice she gave was full of love, truth, and was supported with scriptural background. Since that first encounter, we have had several conversations and prayers together, and even though we have never met in person, the light that is within her travels through each post, prayer, and conversation we share. I truly appreciate the way Rita allows God to lead her daily to share her own personal testimony as an example of God's grace, mercy, and promise to reward those who seek after him diligently. Before, I was hidden in my own sorrows, broken, lost, and hurt by the past decisions I had made in my life. But Hidden & Found helped me to find myself, it was the start to me diving deeper in discovering my purpose, it encouraged me to stand strong while I wait for my Kingdom Purpose Mate to find me, and ultimately being made whole with God. Rita, thank you for your transparency, and for not forgetting about your assignment to single women even though you are married. I love you with the love of the Lord!

—*Bethany Glass*
(now soon to be Baker)

Made in the USA
Columbia, SC
26 October 2021